Ocean Friendly Gardens

H A N D B O O K

Produced by the Surfrider Foundation

Ocean Friendly Gardens: A How-To Gardening Guide to Help Restore a Healthy Coast and Ocean

1st Edition June 2009

Copyright ©2009 Surfrider Foundation

Published by: Surfrider Foundation USA

    San Clemente, CA

    P.O. Box 6010

    San Clemente, CA 92674-6010

    (949) 492-8170; FAX (949) 492-8142

    http://www.surfrider.org/

Author: Douglas Kent

Book Editor: Joe Geever

Front Photos and Illustrations: Douglas Kent and Steve Gunther

Interior Illustrations: Douglas Kent and Richard Kent

Interior Photos: Douglas Kent and Steve Gunther

Book Design and Layout: PMGD, Patty Roberts

Table of Contents

Notes

Foreword

Welcome to Ocean Friendly Gardens!

By Joe Geever
Surfrider Foundation – California Policy Coordinator

Surfrider Foundation initiated this program for our members who want to take some steps at their own homes to reduce pollution reaching our precious ocean. Many of our members are surprised to learn just how much they can help clean up our coastal waterways and ocean water by some simple and beautiful changes to their gardens.

Let me tell you why we organized this manual the way we did.

Several years ago we began researching the idea of Ocean Friendly Gardens and compiling studies that showed the enormous benefits to our environment from proper landscaping and irrigation. Several of us, myself included, decided to convert our own gardens and share that experience with our members.

As with any new subject or skill, there is a harder way and an easier way to learn. The hard way is setting out without any help and enduring a series of mistakes, lessons learned, and changes made. The easier way is to let experienced teachers educate you.

I am not a gardener. But I had the great fortune of meeting Doug Kent, the author of this manual, when he volunteered to lend his considerable expertise to our development of the Ocean Friendly Gardens program. Unfortunately, I met Doug after I converted my garden.

This book is written for gardeners and non-gardeners alike. It is a "How To…" manual to help the reader avoid unnecessary, time-consuming, expensive and frustrating mistakes. It allows inexperienced gardeners (like me) to plan and construct a garden that is beautiful and environmentally-conscious. However, it also provides helpful tips for the more experienced gardener to change the traditional approach to landscaping and incorporate "CPR" (conservation, permeability, retention) into an Ocean Friendly Garden.

We suggest that you use this book like you would use an "Owner's Manual." It is organized and written to help you walk through the process of converting your garden, step by step. It is not a book to read and put on the shelf – it is a tool to refer to repeatedly. Keep it next to you on the kitchen table when you're drawing your plan, scribble in the liner, take it with you in the yard and get it dirty when you're working. Like a pencil and paper, or a shovel and rake – it's a tool.

This book is organized into four straightforward steps: 1) Planning, 2) Preparation, 3) Construction and 4) Maintenance. You'll see that there are considerations of construction and maintenance that you need to understand before you put pencil to paper and plan your garden conversion. And most importantly, you need a plan before you do anything else. Proper planning and preparation helps limit the time and expense of construction and maintenance.

So, how do you use this book? Read it through first to help understand the results of what you're setting out to do. Then go back to the beginning and use it as a guide to a step-by-step process for converting your garden into a beautiful landscape that reflects your taste and respect for nature. Finally, be prepared to lend this book to your neighbors. Our experience is that these beautiful gardens will attract a lot of curiosity – if not envy. Not only can you do your part to restore our coast and ocean – your garden will be an inspiration to your friends and neighbors to do the same.

Again, welcome to Ocean Friendly Gardens.

CHAPTER ONE

Introduction

As a group of people, ocean lovers and gardeners would never intentionally harm an ecosystem. We tend to be a conscientious bunch. This book has been written for this group of people – the people in urban/suburban communities in the U.S. that want to improve the quality of their ocean, bay, river, or lake. It explains how to design, create, and maintain a landscape that does not pollute.

As I write this, I'm sitting at home trying to cough up a pound of junk that has been in my lungs for two weeks. And for the first time in four days, my temperature has finally dropped below 100 degrees.

I've got pneumonia. My doctor said that I got it from exposure to polluted water in the ocean, which means that I'm probably not the only one with a pollution-related health problem. Many surfers, swimmers and other ocean enthusiasts suffer a similar fate.

But our problems don't only exist in the ocean and they don't start there. Human activity has played havoc on the world's water systems, and as the cliché goes, the water is striking back. Algae, bacteria, and who knows what else, are taking over our oceans, lakes, and rivers, fed by an enormous increase in unwelcome nutrients draining off of the land, and nurtured by the continual elimination of natural predators and their habitats. The consequences of this invasion (cough, cough) are widespread and alarming.

CPR is our way of restoring the health of our oceans and waterways – our goal is to either stop or clean polluted runoff. This is something WE ALL can do.

Gardeners truly affect their local waterways, and we do so in two distinct ways.

First, we influence the amount of water running off a landscape. Prior to development, most landscapes absorbed the majority of rainfall. But now between 30% and 80% of an urban/suburban homesite is comprised of impermeable surfaces that block the natural absorption of water. We also make the problem worse by planting vegetation that isn't adapted to the climate we live in. We have to water our yards excessively, and often that irrigation water runs off the property and eventually to our local beach.

Second, we influence the quality of water running off our properties. Water running into the ocean is not inherently harmful, it is the stuff attached to it and the stuff it picks up on the way to the ocean that is. Fertilizers, pesticides, oils, cleaning solutions, and organic debris all run off a landscape. These chemicals and organic substances are the culprits that encourage algae and bacteria.

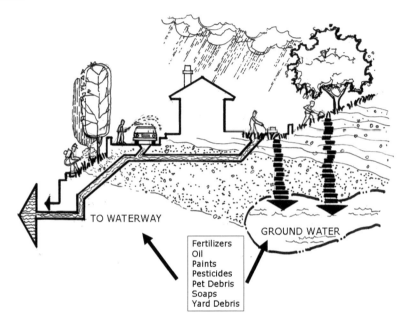

TO WATERWAY

GROUND WATER

Fertilizers
Oil
Paints
Pesticides
Pet Debris
Soaps
Yard Debris

CPR STANDS FOR CONSERVATION, PERMEABILITY, AND RETENTION.

Conserving the use of water, fertilizers, and pesticides not only reduces the amount and improves the quality of water running off a landscape, but helps protect the aquifer that sits below the garden from these pollutants too. Conservation implies being creative; doing the same, but with less. It also means pulling the most out of water and managing fertilizers and pesticides with a willingness to use non- toxic alternatives.

Increasing **permeability** within a landscape allows it to hold more of its water, pollutants, and nutrients, meaning less of this stuff makes its way to the storm drains and eventually to our coastal waterways and ocean. All properties possess opportunities to increase permeability, such as changing pathways, patios, and driveways.

Retaining water mimics natural processes. In many cases retention/infiltration areas help replenish a groundwater aquifer, which directly benefits the communities that rely on groundwater. Retention/infiltration areas are places within a landscape where water is allowed to sit and infiltrate. These devices are important at capturing the first rain event of the season—the event that carries the most pollutants to our ocean.

My doctor said that it will take me months to recover from my bacterial infection. Enough time to finish writing this book, but time away from doing the things I love. While I do not know if water pollution is a problem gardeners can solve all by themselves, we possess the opportunity to change the one thing we have the most control over, our gardens.

I have been creating Ocean Friendly Gardens for many years and as you will see throughout this book, landscapes that incorporate the concepts of CPR are unique and sometimes exceptionally beautiful. Quite possibly, an Ocean Friendly Garden merits the effort solely based on these attributes.

Soon, and like old times, I will be able to a catch a cool swim after a warm and rewarding day in the garden. Something we should all be lucky enough to enjoy. Hopefully, with all of our help, the ocean and bays near where I live can again be healthy enough to accommodate these once regular activities.

Notes

CHAPTER TWO

Designing

CPR is more than a design idea, it is a lifeguard. CPR protects swimmers, marine life and their habitats. Yet unlike a lifeguard, CPR never stops working. It is always on-guard helping to restore life to our oceans, rivers, and lakes.

The goals of CPR, and this book, are simple: runoff is either stopped or cleaned. Conservation, permeability, and retention are the tools employed to reach these goals.

This chapter will help you develop a conceptual landscape plan. The following chapters detail how to execute it. With a little patience, foresight, and experimentation, the average gardener can create a landscape that not only protects the ocean, rivers, and lakes; but is beautiful, useful, and yes, life saving.

STEPS
Get or create a base plan
Develop design layers
Create paths for rain water
Pull it all together

DESIGNING AN OCEAN-FRIENDLY LANDSCAPE – "LAYERING"

It all starts with a "vision" of what you want your garden and surrounding areas to look like. After reading this manual, and getting an idea of the plants and designs that make up an Ocean Friendly Garden, you will be able to identify examples in magazines, websites and in your daily travels.

For those of us with limited experience in landscaping, it is helpful to look at photos of beautiful gardens that exemplify the principles of CPR. Or, when you're traveling around your hometown, keep an eye out for attractive gardens that appeal to you and take your own pho-

Aerial photo of community association: Laguna Niguel, CA, a 10 acre site

The principles of CPR and the methods for design prescribed in this chapter were used to redesign the landscape pictured above. Although not readily apparent, this community now produces far less pollutants, uses less resources, and will continue to improve as the residents adapt to the changes and take pride in their surroundings. The techniques and methods recommended in this chapter and book can be used for any type of landscape, in any type of condition; new or existing, big or small.

tographs. These photos will help you create a "vision" of your future landscape.

Like so many projects in life, having a plan before starting the work is critical to success and will save time and money in the long run. This chapter will help you take the vision of your new landscape and put it on paper – a blueprint for each of the steps necessary for your Ocean Friendly Garden conversion.

Although there are many ways to design a landscape, layering is a method that works well with any type of landscape, new or existing. Layering involves breaking down the processes of design into smaller, more manageable parts (layers). The four layers of designing an ocean friendly landscape are: 1) identifying function and use, 2) documenting the three key water areas, 3) providing paths for runoff, and lastly, 4) pulling it all together.

GETTING STARTED

In order for layering to work a site plan will be needed. A site plan is a drawing of your property with all the major features on it, such as the house, trees, and driveway. If your house did not come with a site plan, then you will have to measure the property yourself and draw a basic site plan.

First, measure the perimeter of your property with a tape measure. You don't need to measure inches – the perimeter measured in feet is detailed enough. Then go to an office supply store and buy a "flip chart" or a couple sheets of "poster board" (preferably with a 1-inch grid printed on the page), a roll of tracing paper (as wide as the flip chart), a yard stick, and dark pencils. The 1-inch grid on the flip chart page will allow you to "scale" your drawing. For example, if the perimeter of your property is 60 feet by 90 feet, and the flip chart page is 25 inches by 30 inches, then you may choose a conversion factor of "1 inch equals 3 feet" for your drawing. If the store doesn't have poster board or flip charts with a grid printed on the sheet, no worries – you can draw in "hash marks" on the edges to make the measuring simpler.

Once you draw the property lines on your site plan, measure and draw in the outside of the house and its distance from the property lines, and then measure and place any feature you intend to keep in your new design (such as the driveway, sidewalk, patios, walkways, trees).

Once the site plan is completed, tracing paper is used for the following layers. Each layer discussed below is followed by an illustration, which may be similar to the drawing you produce.

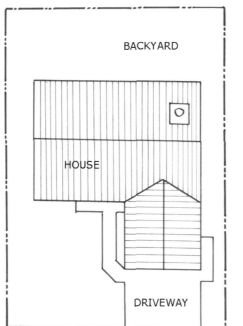

Your site plan may look like this example,

LAYER 1: IDENTIFY FUNCTION AND USE

For an ocean friendly garden to succeed, it must also be human friendly.

First, make a list of requirements. Do you need additional living and entertaining space? Do you want a safe and durable place for your children or pets to play? … Maybe your priority is an aesthetically pleasing sanctuary in which to relax and recharge? …Privacy? ….Fresh produce and herbs? …All of the above?

Second, you need to make distinctions between high and low use areas. Safety is the priority in high use areas, such as walkways and playing spaces. Permeability is the priority in low use areas. Once you have prioritized the functions of your new landscape, you can place a sheet of tracing paper over your "site plan" and draw your first layer – the high use and low use areas of the garden. The byproduct of this layer (function and use) is a landscape that captures your interest, invites your use, and yet isolates costs and impervious surfaces.

One tip — an area identified for high use, like play spaces or entertainment areas, may double as retention areas during rainy weather. This cross-over area, and others, will be a consideration in the next "layer."

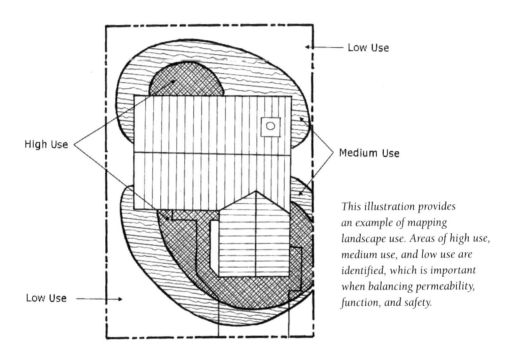

This illustration provides an example of mapping landscape use. Areas of high use, medium use, and low use are identified, which is important when balancing permeability, function, and safety.

LAYER 2: IDENTIFY THE THREE KEY WATER AREAS

The next layer of design is identifying the three key water areas of a landscape. An important consideration for visualizing the Three Key Water Areas is gravity. To link the three areas into the design, try to imagine rain water running from high spots and impermeable surfaces to a retention area – and possibly beyond. The progression of the moving water should be outlined in your drawing by connecting:

        1 · DRAINAGE — areas that must drain and be kept dry

        2 · INFILTRATION — areas that can retain water

        3 · EXIT — areas where runoff can exit a landscape

Drainage Areas

There are many places on a property that need to be kept dry by diverting water away. Moisture building up around foundations, patios, and decks can cause rot and mold problems – and expensive repairs. Also, the pathways leading from doors should be kept dry for safety reasons and areas used for storage should always be kept moisture-free to prevent damage to your belongings.

Infiltration Areas

While certain areas in your landscape should remain dry, others can collect the water that would otherwise run off the property and potentially pollute our local streams, rivers, wetlands and ocean. In these areas water percolates into the soil. Properly identifying these areas is important because retaining water in other locations of a landscape may actually increase erosion and the chance of topsoil loss and soil slips. If your property is on a slope greater than 20 percent, please refer to Chapter 12.

An effective retention/infiltration area should possess these characteristics:
- It should be located on slopes no greater than 20 percent.
- It should not sit immediately uphill of a steep or moderately steep slope (anything greater than 20%).
- It should be easy to access and maintain.
- It should provide a safe exit for overflowing water.
- It should be able to support vigorously growing plants.

Infiltration areas can almost be any size. Naturally, though, the larger the area, the more polluted runoff it can hold.

Exit Areas

Not all water can be retained in a landscape. At some point, some amount of water – whether from extreme rains or property-related chores – will exit a property. And with it will run off topsoil, plant debris, and pollutants. This exiting water can be managed, and to some degree, sediment and pollutants can be removed with screening/cleaning devices. The area needed to support screening/cleaning devices does not have to be large. For a more thorough explanation of screening and cleaning runoff before it leaves your property, refer to Chapter 11.

The area selected to manage exiting water should have these characteristics:
- It should be located as close to the property line as possible, and it should be the last thing the runoff hits on its way off the property.
- It should have good accessibility, because the debris it collects will need to be cleaned out.
- The area and screening device should be able to direct overflowing water (usually caused by a clog or extra-heavy rainfall) to a safe place, such as a gutter or another drainage system. The runoff leaving an exit area should not cause a problem to surrounding properties.

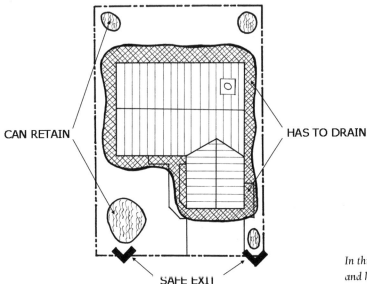

CAN RETAIN

HAS TO DRAIN

SAFE EXIT

LAYER 3: PROVIDE PATHS FOR RUNOFF

The third layer of design links the three key landscape areas together. In this step, you create paths for runoff. A water path usually starts from areas that need good drainage (and thus have high runoff), such as roofs and driveways; leads water to retention areas by way of permeable surfaces; and, if needed, safely allows water to exit the landscape via special devices and storm drains. Among the many devices, water can be transported by pipes, channels, culverts, swales, and dry creek beds.

Roofs, driveways, and sidewalk strips require special attention because of the large amount of runoff they produce.

Roofs

Of the total property, roofs can occupy a significant amount of space. For example, in Huntington Beach, California, the average residential roof size is about 2,300 square feet; on an average lot size of about 6,200 square feet: 37 percent of the total area. The percentage of roof is often greater in newer developments because lot sizes tend to be smaller and homes larger than in older neighbor-

In this example roof and house water runs into gutters that lead to underground pipes which pop out at retention basins. In case of deluge, runoff safely exits to the street.

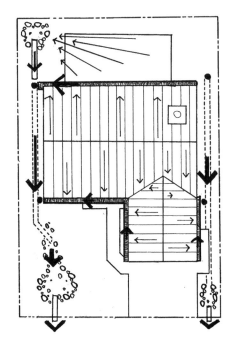

hoods. Huntington Beach receives an average of 11.9 inches of rainfall a year and at this rate, the average roof annually sheds about 15,354 gallons of rainwater (accounting for a 10 percent loss due to evaporation). During a 1-inch rain event, the roof will shed 1,290 gallons.

CALCULATING AMOUNT OF RAINWATER

Calculating the amount of water that falls on a surface is easy. If, for example, 1 inch of rain fell on a 1 square foot box, then the box would have 0.623 gallons of rainwater inside of it. However, there is a difference between the amount of water that falls on a surface and the amount of water that runs off. Evaporation creates the difference, and for this equation 10% of all the water that falls on a surface is subtracted, due to evaporation. Use the simple steps below to calculate the amount of water falling on your property, driveway or roof.

1. **Area of driveway, roof, or any surface is Length x Width = _____ sq. ft.**
2. **Multiply the area by 0.55 * = _____ gallons of water per inch of rain**
3. **Multiply that amount of water by the amount of rain in inches = _____ gallons of water. This is the total amount of water falling on and possibly running off a surface.**

* Actual amount is 0.623 , but due to evaporation and loss, the amount of water actually collected will be less, hence 0.55

Runoff from roofs is slightly different than the water coming out of the tap. Because it comes from rain, roof water is typically soft, meaning that it lacks calcium carbonates. It can also have a lot of debris and particulates, and may be laden with the nitrogenous by-products, such as ammonium and nitrate, from the exhaust of cars, buses, airplanes and other combustion engines. These substances are extremely damaging to the marine environment. But, they often can be absorbed into the soil with few ill effects -- in fact, plants fare better with soft water and added nitrogen. Your landscape should be designed to capture and use roof water for the health of the garden, or at least screen and/or clean it before it reaches the street.

When managing roof water, there are four goals. First, get the water away from the house. A dry house is a healthier house. Second, slow and diffuse the water, allowing sediment to drop out. Third, try to filter the water by diverting it to heavily planted areas. And lastly, if roof water can not be run through the landscape to remove nutrients and sediment, then at least run it though a filter, such as a gravel bed or cloth (refer to Chapter 11), before it exits the property. If possible, do not run roof water across impermeable surfaces, such as a driveway, because it will pick up more sediment and pollutants before exiting.

A roof without gutters poses particular challenges. If the eaves do not overhang an impermeable surface, such as concrete, then the water can cause considerable damage to the soil below, compacting it, causing small gullies and ensuring runoff. Two strategies for overcoming this wall of water are to put a gravel walkway underneath the eaves or to place durable plants that can withstand falling water and diffuse it.

While roof water that is channeled by gutters and downspouts is more manageable than a roof without gutters, these systems also present challenges: the water flow is so quick and concentrated that it is typically funneled right off the property. Diffusing this fast-moving water is the key to managing it. A diffusion device is offered below.

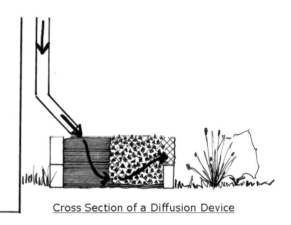

These two illustrations show a gutter diffusion box. This easy constructed device removes debris and slows fast moving roof runoff.

Cross Section of a Diffusion Device

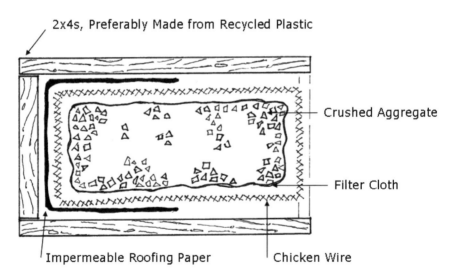

2x4s, Preferably Made from Recycled Plastic

Crushed Aggregate

Filter Cloth

Impermeable Roofing Paper   Chicken Wire

Facing page top, is an illustration of a landscape in Los Angeles and its two different approaches used to manage the roof runoff. One of the methods directs the water from a gutter straight into aggressive ground cover and a small mound, which slows the water, allowing the sediment to drop out. The other method captures the water sheeting from the driveway and directs it, via an underground pipe, to a swale that leads to an infiltration area.

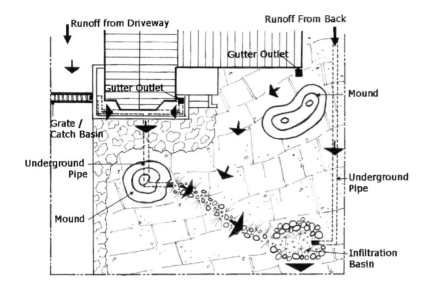

An illustration of an actual garden shows how runoff is managed. This garden captures over 12,000 gallons of polluted runoff a year.

The labels in the illustration read:

Runoff from Driveway
Runoff From Back
Gutter Outlet
Gutter Outlet
Mound
Grate / Catch Basin
Underground Pipe
Underground Pipe
Mound
Infiltration Basin

Driveways

A 300- to 400-square-foot driveway is fairly common. If, for example, your driveway is 350 square feet, and you receive 15 inches of rainfall a year, then the driveway will shed about 2,945 gallons of water annually (minus a 10 percent loss to evaporation). If the driveway is used for parking, then the runoff produced from it will be high in oils and dust. An ocean friendly garden will divert driveway runoff to the garden, where some of the pollutants can be filtered out.

Sidewalk Strip / Parkway

Turf is commonly used in the long, narrow landscapes that sit between sidewalks and streets. Like few other ground covers, turf can tolerate the heavy foot traffic and pollutants these landscapes must endure. The trade-off is a high-maintenance ground cover that results in overspray from the irrigation system and runoff that can be loaded with fertilizers and debris. Luckily, there are many ways to create non-polluting parkways.

A successful parkway will provide paths that direct people from their cars to the sidewalk. Around the pathways, use plants that can tolerate occasional traffic, and are kind to the people that pass them.

To reach these goals, build flat, permeable, and easily-navigated foot pads every 2 to 3 feet, which can be made from pavers, bricks, or stone with a flat surface. Or, go the extra mile and re-use pieces of concrete from a demolition project (reducing your cost and eliminating material sent to the landfill).

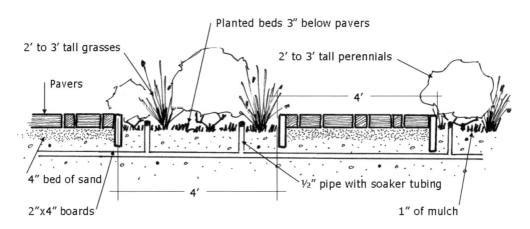

Practical Parkways / Sidewalk Strips

To set these materials, dig a shallow trench (several inches deeper than the depth of the paver material) where the pathway will go. Partially fill the trench with sand or decomposed granite. Then push the stone down with the weight of your body until the sand forms around the bottom of the stone or paver, and the surface is the same height as the curb and sidewalk. Finally, remove the paver to fill any voids in the sand base. You may need to repeat this process several times to ensure the paver is flat and secure – safe to walk on for years to come. Once the stone or pavers are secure, either fill the gaps with more sand or decomposed granite, or plant durable low-growing groundcover between the pavers. Large pavers or flat stones can be spaced several inches apart to allow room for groundcover, but still provide a safe and attractive walkway.

Knee-high plants are used in between the foot paths (anything lower and people will be inclined to march right through the plants). The vegetation used in sidewalk strips is unique because it must be the most human friendly (no irritants or thorns), yet incredibly durable, and in many situations can be drought adapted – requiring limited watering to maintain their health and beauty. These planted beds sit 2 to 3 inches below the pavers and sidewalk, making them an effective trap for runoff.

The last component of an ocean friendly parkway is its irrigation system. Soaker hose and inline tubing are low-maintenance options that not only prevent overspray, but can tolerate being stepped on, too.

LAYER 4: PULL IT ALL TOGETHER

The last step in creating a conceptual plan for an ocean friendly landscape is pulling all the layers together in a master plan. So far you should have a "site plan", a drawing on tracing paper of your high and low use areas, a separate sheet with your 3 key water areas, and finally a sheet with the pathways for rain water (including your parkway plan). To pull all the layers together, cut a final sheet of blank tracing paper, place it on the site plan and make a copy with a dark pencil. Then place it on the "3 water areas" and line up the site plan – then trace the water areas onto the master plan. Repeat this process to incorporate the water pathways and parkway plan onto the master plan sheet.

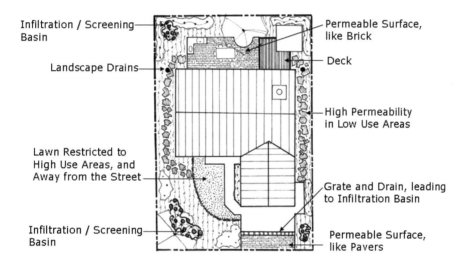

The following chapters will help you select the right plants and materials for your situation. When human function, the three key landscape/water areas, and the unique aspects of roofs and driveways are combined, your landscape plan may look something like the illustration above.

IDEAS TO PLAN ON

Your Ocean Friendly Garden should be unique in design and plant selection, reflecting your creativity and creating a place you and others can enjoy. In this section are some of the elements that will help you design a landscape that either captures runoff or cleans it. These recommendations can be incorporated into beautiful and distinctive gardens – in fact, they create beauty and distinction.

Contours and Curves: The ability of water to run off a property is related to the number of obstacles in its path. The more obstacles there are, the less runoff. Creating an undulating ground surface, however slight, will minimize runoff. And if possible, put curves in pathways, which break up straight lines and help prevent sheeting water from ever gaining enough momentum to do damage.

Compost: While compost does indeed happen naturally, in an urban/suburban environment compost needs space and sometimes a little encouragement. When designing your landscape allocate no less than 1% of the property to composting. A 6,200 sq. ft. lot, for example, will need to set aside about 60 sq. ft. (an area 10' by 6'), and a 12,000 sq. ft. property needs a 120 sq. ft. composting area. To speed and enhance the processes of compost, put the pile in a warm location, create easy access, and plumb a water line or garden hose to it.

Lawns: For functional and aesthetic reasons, you may not want to remove all of your lawn in favor of more ecologically friendly alternatives. But you can isolate a lawn and the pollutants it creates from the street and storm drain. Lawns should be placed closest to where people will walk on them, such as around entryways. Lawns used for play areas should ideally be located away from the perimeter of the garden to allow a buffer for capturing the pollutants and excess water before it reaches the street.

Trees and Shrubs: Although turf is fairly good at slowing and stopping runoff (at least better than most walking surfaces), trees, shrubs, and ground covers are far better – up to 30% to 50% more runoff and rain is captured in landscapes planted with trees, shrubs, and ground covers, as opposed to lawns. And not only do these plants require less fertilizer (and water) than turf, they also pull pollutants from the soil, water, and atmosphere, while harboring more wildlife.

Watering: Using water is OK – water is an amazing resource. Unlike a vast majority of the resources brought into a landscape, such as pesticides, concrete, and machinery, the energy used to get water to a landscape can be offset by the energy and carbon dioxide captured by the plants through photosynthesis. The goal for gardeners is to maximize this resource, pulling the greatest benefit from it, while using it as efficiently as possible. Water is beneficial, and through its use an urban/suburban environment can be improved with more trees, more flowers, more food, and yet, still produce less polluted runoff.

Plan on Pee: In urban and suburban neighborhoods dogs and their walkers are as much a part of the environment as kids, cars and cranky neighbors. Instead of lamenting dogs peeing in, or around your garden, create a spot for them to go – plant a pee pole. A pee pole will not only divert dogs from peeing on more favorable plants, but may also be able to keep their nitrogen-rich fluids from entering the storm drain system. A few of the many plants that can tolerate dog's urine include calla lily, Carex pansa, clover, Juncus, and papyrus.

Diversity: Creating a landscape that is diverse, both in plant selections and ground covering, provides a slew of benefits. A diverse range of plants will lower maintenance costs by reducing the need for expensive resources, such as gasoline, fertilizers, and pesticides. Like a wildland, a diverse range of plants creates a symbiotic mini-ecosystem where no one particular nutrient is pulled from the ground faster than it can be naturally replaced. The effects of harmful pests, such as bugs and weeds, are also reduced in a landscape with a wide range of

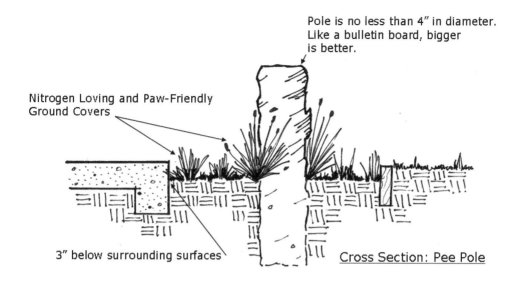

Pole is no less than 4" in diameter.
Like a bulletin board, bigger
is better.

Nitrogen Loving and Paw-Friendly
Ground Covers

3" below surrounding surfaces

Cross Section: Pee Pole

plants; a bug's predator is encouraged to visit and weeds are choked out by natural competition. Ground surfaces should be dynamic too. Concrete may run from a door and change to pavers, which might then transition to turf blocks, eventually leading to mulched pathways (see Chapter 8). Diversity is as good for a healthy watershed as it is for beauty and whimsy.

Notes

3

Plants

Plants are dynamic. They can not only stop or clean runoff, plants can nourish, cool, protect, and for some, even provide endless delight. Naturally, picking the right plant, for the right spot, will help ensure less runoff, as well as provide more nourishment, protection, and delight.

Two more design layers are needed for plant selection. The first layer defines microclimates, areas that differ in amount of sun and water. The second layer highlights the functions that plants must perform, such as screening a neighbor or shading a house.

To start, pull out your site plan again and get ready to repeat the drafting process from Chapter 2.

STEPS
Identifying Microclimates
Understand Your Soil Moisture
Select Individual Plants

IDENTIFYING MICROCLIMATES
Sun

Every landscape has different microclimates. For the most part, the amount of sun is what makes these microclimates differ. For purposes of plant selection and irrigation, microclimates can be divided into three broad categories: full sun, partial sun, and shade.

Full sun means that the area gets 6 or more hours of direct sunlight a day; partial sun means between 3 to 6 hours of direct sun; and shade equals 3 hours or less of direct sun.

Notably, there are places within a landscape, because of surrounding features like houses and trees, which may get full sun in the summer, but be in total shade in the winter (see example below). These areas need to be identified on your drawing to ensure planting success. As before, use a sheet of tracing paper, on top of the site plan, to trace in your existing structures and add the sunlight areas.

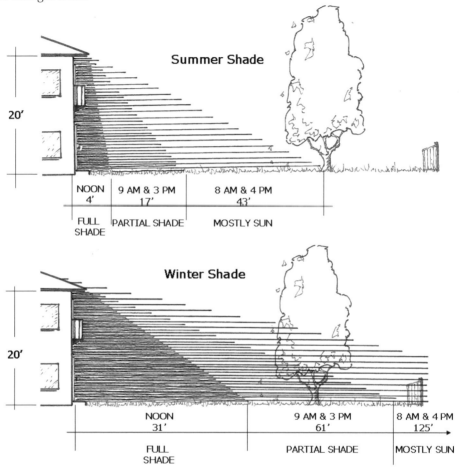

After analyzing your property you may find a lot of variation in the amount of sunlight. The plan you develop may look something like the illustration above.

Understand Your Soil Moisture

Moisture levels within a landscape will vary, sometimes significantly. The amount of difference can greatly influence the type of plants that will most likely succeed in your landscape.

Dry wooden dowels are the only tool needed to check soil moisture. In areas throughout your landscape, drive the dry wooden dowels 1 foot into the ground. Let the dowel stay in the ground for 20 seconds. The dowel will clearly show the changes of moisture from depth, and a soil's relative amount of water; the darker the wood, the more moisture.

If possible, probe the soil in late spring, when the top two inches of soil is completely dry, but before the irrigation system has been turned back on for the dry season. It is common to find areas within a landscape that are still quite moist.

Again, draw the areas of higher and lower moisture content on the sheet of tracing paper with the areas of sunlight exposure.

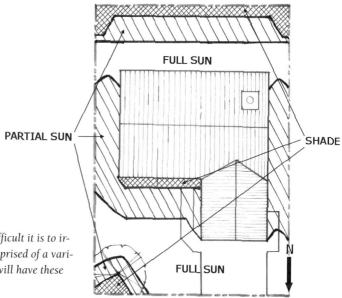

The illustration above shows how difficult it is to irrigate properly – the property is comprised of a variety of microclimates. Your property will have these variations too.

IDENTIFYING FUNCTIONAL USES FOR PLANTS

Using your plot plan, head back into your landscape and begin listing the roles plants must play in your landscape.

Here is a list of the many functions plants can assume in our landscapes. The plant can: live without excessive use of water; grow and be healthy without chemical fertilizers and pesticides; help passively cool (shade) and heat (insulate) your home; screen neighbors from peering into your private spaces; attract wildlife, such as birds and butterflies; help stop unwanted people and pets from coming into your landscape; help stop unwanted weed seeds from blowing into your landscape; provide food or useful materials; and importantly, help remove pollutants from runoff.

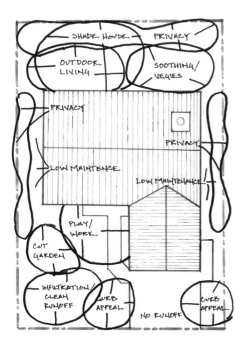

Plants can perform many needed functions, but in order for them to work these functions must be listed and laid out.

SELECTING INDIVIDUAL PLANTS

There are hundreds of books, articles, and websites dedicated to helping you choose the right plant for each situation. Instead of competing with this existing work, this book focuses on plants that will protect our oceans and waterways. These include alternatives to lawns, nitrogen-fixing plants (which reduce the need for fertilizers), plants that can effectively hold hills; plants for infiltration areas; and lastly plants to avoid (those aquatic and terrestrial invasive species that can degrade a natural environment). A list of diverse plants for each purpose in each region of the country is available at www.surfrider.org/ofg.

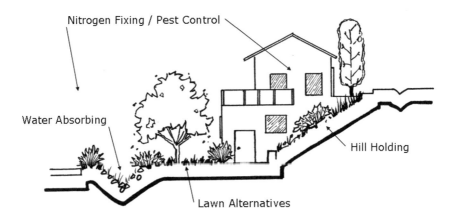

TIPS

Dry on the Outside: Use plants with low water needs on the outskirts of your property. The outskirts are where runoff will most likely occur and keeping these areas dry helps slow/stop wet season runoff; and the low flow irrigation system used to water these areas will produce little or no dry season runoff.

Increase Diversity: A diverse range of plants will decrease the amount of damage from pest infestations, if not deter them altogether. Diversity can also lower the need for fertilizers (no one nutrient is grossly consumed). There is a natural beauty to diversity too, and many people find the variation in size, shape, color and texture to be visually appealing and soothing. Your choice and placement of plants can reflect your character and artistic side while livening up your neighborhood.

Promote Good Air Circulation: During a particular time of year, or in a particular place within a garden, things can get muggy, creating the conditions favorable for fungus, disease, and a variety of pests. Sooty mold, spider mites, and mealy-bugs thrive in landscapes with high humidity and poor air circulation. As a design solution, ample space must be provided between trees and shrubs, and they should not be allowed to grow into each other.

Be Aware of Shade: It is easy to underestimate the amount of shade in a landscape. Landscapes in older communities, those with larger trees and shrubs, may be entirely in shade. Six hours of uninterrupted sun in the summer constitutes the minimum needs of a plant requiring full sun. A plant requiring full sun but grown in shade will perform poorly, and may have sparse foliage, be more prone to pest infestations, and its fruit and flowers will be lackluster. If an area does not get 6 hours of full sun, then use plants requiring shade.

CHAPTER FOUR

Irrigation

The functional elements of your landscape have been decided and the type of plants selected – now it's time to design the irrigation system. This chapter will help you design an efficient irrigation system, one that does not over-water, over-spray, or demand excessive maintenance.

The first step is to consider the entire irrigation system, from the main valve manifold to the watering devices that are most appropriate for the plants and soils in different areas of the garden. At first glance, the multiple considerations of an irrigation system can seem overwhelming. Don't be discouraged – with patience and creativity you can design and build a beautiful garden with limited irrigation demands and complications.

Next we take a step back and draft a design layer that allows you to lay out the valve manifold assembly, the underground supply lines, and the "lateral lines" that deliver water to the individual watering devices – what is called "roughing in the plumbing." This plan "layer" will assist you in roughing in the irrigation system (Chapter 7) as well as completing the final touches to the irrigation system (Chapter 9). Our end goal is to ensure that, once the garden is completed, the finishing touches to the irrigation system will be in the right place to do the job properly.

STEPS
Determine Hydrozones
Select Type of Watering Device for Each Hydrozone
Determine the Proper Spacing between Watering Devices

DETERMINING HYDROZONES
A hydrozone is an area comprised of plants with the same watering needs. A hydrozone exists

within a microclimate (discussed in previous chapter) and there may be several hydrozones within a microclimate. For example, a native landscape and vegetable garden represent two completely different hydrozones; one requiring deep and infrequent water, and the other shallow and frequent; yet both hydrozones may be in the same microclimate: full sun, with dry, clay soil.

For sake of simplicity, your landscape can be divided into the following 5 plant categories (1. annuals, 2. turf & ground covers, 3. Densely-planted perennials and shrubs, 4. large shrubs, and 5. trees) mixed into the 3 micro-climates identified in the previous chapter (full sun, partial sun, shade) creating possibly 15 total hydrozones. As illustrated below, the combination of sun and water needs can reduce the number of valves to six or less.

1) Low growing ground cover; full sun; regular water.
2) Medium shrubs; partial sun, low water.
3) Retention Areas: perennials; full sun; regular water.
4) Large shrubs and tree; full sun; low water.
5) Perennials and low shrubs; partial sun; low water.
6) Low growing ground cover; shade; low water.

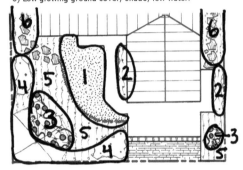

The hydrozones are highlighted in the base plan used in the previous chapters.

SELECTING TYPE OF WATERING DEVICE

While there are many different watering devices, most can fall into one of the two categories below:

1) Overhead Sprinkler Devices

Rotor Spray Heads: The most efficient device for overhead water delivery, these devices have internal gears that help produce an even stream of water. Because water is delivered at a lower rate, the amount of time these devices are run is greater than overhead spray heads.

Spray Heads: Possibly the most common type of watering device in residential landscapes, overhead spray heads can provide even coverage, but deliver a lot of water in a short amount of time, making them ideally suited for lawns and low growing ground covers. Spray heads are not recommended for steep slopes and dense soils.

Impact Spray Heads: The least water efficient type of sprinklers heads, these devices are not recommended for an ocean friendly garden.

2) Low Flow Devices

Drip: Micro-sprayers, bubblers, and emitters are all part of the drip system. While they are exceptionally efficient, they can be maintenance needy, making them ideal for small and/or highly accessible areas.

Soaker Hose: Oozing water along its entire length, soaker hose is fairly efficient, easy to install, and does not demand a lot of maintenance. Soaker hose is ideal for densely planted areas because it delivers a lot of water (for a low flow device). It can, however, deliver too much water for steep slopes and dense soils. A pressure reducer must be used with soaker hose.

Inline Soaker Tubing: Tubing with emitters installed at measured intervals, inline tubing is the lowest maintenance and most efficient low flow watering device. These devices are ideally suited for slopes, dense soils, and drought-adapted landscapes.

RULE OF THUMB

> **Annuals:** Low flow soaker hose.
> **Turfgrass and ground covers:** overhead sprinklers, such as rotor and spray heads.
> **Densely planted perennials and shrubs:** low flow soaker hose.
> **Large shrubs:** Low flow drip and inline tubing.
> **Trees:** Low flow drip, soaker hose and inline tubing.

SLOPES

Every problem on flat land is magnified on slopes: erosion and runoff are more likely; proper watering is difficult; and the work on slopes takes longer and is harder.

To determine the right type of irrigation system means knowing the degree of your slope. Chapter 12 has an illustration that can help you determine your degree.

SELECTING A WATERING DEVICE FOR SLOPES

As a general rule, slopes with densely planted ground covers and shrubs, (no taller than 2 feet), benefit the most from overhead sprinklers, because they provide the best coverage with the lowest maintenance. However, steep and sparsely-planted slopes, those with large shrubs, and/or slopes with heavy clay soils will benefit the most from a low flow watering device, like inline tubing, and short repetitive water cycles.

The chart below can also help you determine the best type of watering devices for your slope.

Degree	0 to 8%		9% to 16%		17% to 24%		greater than 25%	
Soil Type	cover	bare	cover	bare	cover	bare	cover	bare
sand	S, R	S, R	S, R	S, R	R	R	R	R, L, S
silt/high organics	S, R	S, R	R	R	R	D, L, S	D, L, S	L, S
clay	S, R	R	R	D, L, S	D, L, S	L, S	L	L

LEGEND: S: *overhead spray head.* **R:** *overhead rotor spray head.* **D:** *drip.* **L:** *inline soaker tubing.* **S:** *soaker hose.*

DETERMING THE SPACING OF WATERING DEVICES

The spacing of overhead sprinklers is fairly straight forward. Low flow devices, on the other hand, require a balanced understanding of your soil and watering device.

Overhead sprinkler heads are generally spaced so that they overlap. Sprinkler heads that throw water 15 feet are spaced 15 feet apart. However, in windy areas (even mildly), spacing should be 80% of throw distance: 15 foot heads are 12 feet apart. Impact sprinkler heads, although not recommended, can be spaced 120% from throw distance: 15 foot throw equals 18 feet apart. In windy communities never place an overhead sprinkler head near impervious surfaces, where the wind in likely to take the water and cause runoff.

Low flow devices rely on the horizontal movement of water and do not demand overlap, like overhead sprinklers. The composition of soil greatly influences horizontal movement; the denser the soil, the greater the movement and distance between water devices. The information below will help you determine your type of soil and the spacing for various devices.

Notably, low flow emitters leave most of the soil looking dry. However, if the watering devices are properly spaced and used, then the soil will be evenly moist just a few inches below the surface

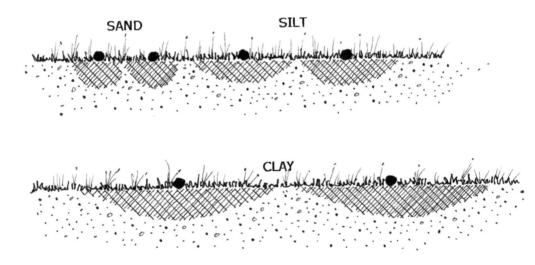

SAND   SILT

CLAY

Type of Soil

Determining the types of soils in your landscape is relatively easy.

1. At various locations throughout your landscape, dig up a handful of soil 6 inches deep.

2. Divide each handful of soil into two clumps and moisten one of them.

3. While still separated by their various locations, grab each soil clump and firmly squeeze.

4. Use the chart below to identify the type of soil of each squeezed clump.

Description	Type of Soil
When wet or dry the soil clumps are loose and easily crumbles apart.	Sand / Course Soil
When dry the soil crumbles, but when moist it reluctantly holds its shape.	Silt / Medium Soil & Soils High in Organic Matter
When dry the soil breaks in to smaller chunks, and when moist easily holds its shape.	Clay / Fine Soil

Device	Sandy	Silt / Organic	Clay
Soaker Hose	1.5'	2'	2.5'
Inline Tubing: 18" apart	X	1'	1.5'
Inline Tubing: 12" apart	1'	1.5'	2'
Emitter: 2gph	1'	1.5'	X
Emitter: ½gph	X	1	1.5'

1) 6" Pop-Up Rotor Spray Heads, 12' apart
2) Soaker Hose, 2' apart
3) Soaker Tubing, 2' apart
4) Inline Soaker Tubing, 1.5' apart
5) Inline Soaker Tubing, 1.5' apart
6) Soaker Hose, 2' apart

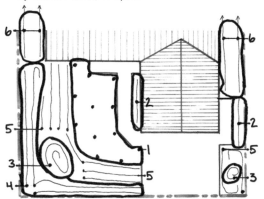

Your irrigation plan may look like this illustration, and possess a variety of irrigation devices. This example landscape was designed for silt soil.

TIPS

Keep it Simple! A good irrigation system will not only last at least 10 years, but also be adaptable to changes in the landscape. The best way to ensure longevity and adaptability is simplicity – the more complicated an irrigation system the more likely it will fail.

Low Flow around Perimeter: Over-spray and dry season runoff are common in landscapes where overhead water devices are used along the perimeter of a landscape, shooting water from errant heads onto the sidewalks and streets. Instead, plan on using low flow devices around the outside of your property (see the previous chapter for planting design ideas).

CHAPTER FIVE

Removing Turf Naturally

Turf demands a large amount of water, fertilizers and attention; all of which have a large impact on the environment. Turf is also the most expensive ground cover to maintain. Removing turf where it doesn't serve a purpose will help the environment and save time and money – a win, win, win idea.

However, removing turf is not quick or easy. Bluegrass, Bermuda, Crab, Devil's, Fescue, Goosegrass, Nut Sedge, Quackgrass, St. Augustine, and Velvetgrass are incredibly tenacious.

This chapter will help you to reclaim an area from unwanted grasses for good, and without the use of herbicides. If herbicides will be used, then the tips following the methods will improve your chances of success. Notably, complete reclamation can take as long as two years. Follow-through is essential and diligence is required – especially until your chosen plants have matured and can compete with the aggressive grasses. The techniques below will work for other unwanted weeds as well.

STEPS
Determine the best method for reclamation
Use tips for success

METHODS FOR RECLAMATION

The differences between the three methods listed below are the amount of time until you can replant, and the amount of resources—such as machinery—that will be needed.

Strip and Pull: "No Till"

This is one of the least expensive, soil nourishing, and quickest techniques. It is a no till method, meaning that the soil never gets turned over, preserving a soil's ecology. Many people have had success with this method.

First, rent a stripper and remove the surface vegetation, which is then composted. For the next two weeks water the area, encouraging the grasses to re-sprout, at which time they are scrapped off the surface with a hoe, or pulled. The area can be graded and planted after this first flush of growth has been removed. Weeding, either by pulling or hoeing, will be needed every two weeks for the first three months, and then once a month thereafter.

Sheet Mulch

If you are in no hurry and aiming for rich soil, then sheet mulching is the technique for you. Completely cover the area with a thick layer of mulch, no less than six inches. The mulch smothers and suffocates the turf. Let the area lie fallow for six months, at which point it can either be tilled or planted. The enormous amount of mulch needed can make this technique cost-prohibitive for large areas. For example, a 500 square foot lawn will require 250 cubic feet of mulch, or 9.3 cubic yards, which requires a fairly large dump truck. Some municipalities and tree companies give mulch away.

Sheet and Till

Opposed to sheeting, this method does not demand as much mulch and the area can be planted sooner. However, it is the most energy intensive method, demanding the use of machines in three steps.

Mow the grass as low as possible and then till the entire area. Spread a two inch layer of mulch and allow the area to sit for three weeks. Water the area periodically to encourage new sprouts. After the three week waiting period, till the new sprouts and mulch into the soil. The area can then be graded, rolled and planted.

HERBICIDES

Although not recommended, many people will choose herbicides because of the convenience. For the sake of human and environmental health, there are a number of steps that can be taken to reduce the ill-effects of herbicides. These steps will also increase efficiency.

- *The turf should be as healthy as possible.* If grass is unhealthy or injured, then its ability to transport the chemical throughout its root system is hindered, lowering the chances of complete dieback. Growing healthy turf may include watering and lightly fertilizing the area.
- *Never use herbicides* around aquatic environments, which can cause a variety of serious problems.
- *Never apply a herbicide when rain is forecasted,* and turn off the automatic irrigation system before applying the herbicides. Hand water if necessary.
- *Never spray herbicides when it is windy,* even slightly. Always wear protective clothing when applying herbicides, which includes long pants, long-sleeved shirt, waterproof

gloves, and protective eyeglasses.

- ***Importantly, do not rush the procedure*** – the goal is it to do it right the first time, avoiding a second or third application.

TIPS

Timing: Late winter and early spring are the best times to remove turf. Both warm and cool season grasses are just taking off. The soil is also easy to work in. A landscape will recover quicker when nourished by the lengthening days and gentle rains expected in mid to late spring.

Ecology: Bacteria, bugs and plants co-exist in a garden; hurt one and others show signs. When working in a landscape, great care should be taken to minimize damage to these important residents. Protect plants from falling and dragged debris. Lay boards and plywood over beds and good soils to distribute the weight of repeated foot steps. If working in dry conditions a light watering will help bind the soil, dampening the dust. Never, ever, work in soggy soil!—it will compact the soil and degrade its health and permeability.

Notes

CHAPTER SIX

Site Preparation and Grading

Finally – the design is finished and you have removed unwanted vegetation – now is the time to dig in and create your ocean friendly garden. As you laid it out in your master plan (from Chapter One), the goal is to end up with contours, water courses, and retention areas. These design elements will reduce runoff from your landscape and the pollutants it carries. Importantly, proper practices will ensure you meet these goals during this construction phase.

With the aid of this chapter you should be able to protect your community from the processes of construction, save and protect your existing topsoil, grade so that the soil stays where you put it, and restore degraded soils.

STEPS
Stop dust and sediment from leaving your property
Protect your topsoil
Grade
Invigorate compacted soils

STOPPING RUNOFF AND DUST DURING CONSTRUCTION
Construction is a dynamic and dirty process – dust will fly, soil is moved about, and water is sometimes used where it won't be captured on-site. Some of this dust, dirt and water will migrate off your property, contributing to ocean and air pollution – but the amount is up to you.

Below are the most commonly used and economically feasible ideas and techniques that stop or reduce the amount of dust, dirt and runoff that leaves your property during construction.

Reducing Sediment Laden Runoff

Protect Storm Drain Inlets: Even before construction begins, defensive measures should be taken to protect against sediments entering the storm drain inlet. Materials used to protect inlets include fiber rolls, gravel, and sandbags.

Create a Staging Area: The dirty parts of construction, such as concrete mixing, sawing and painting, should be concentrated in one area, as opposed to being distributed throughout a landscape. The staging area should never be on the perimeter of your property.

Sandbags: If runoff is a serious problem, then sandbags will be needed to make temporary walls that will hold the water long enough for the sediment to settle out. Normally, these small walls are built along a property's perimeter.

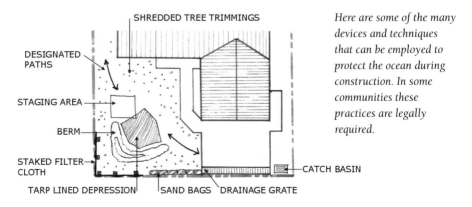

Here are some of the many devices and techniques that can be employed to protect the ocean during construction. In some communities these practices are legally required.

Retention Areas: The water from washing concrete mixers and paint brushes needs to go somewhere. Channel this polluted water to a small retention area within the landscape. When the area dries, then the unwanted material can be swept up and disposed of.

Clean Regularly: All the debris and sediment that ends up in community areas, like sidewalks and streets, should be swept up at the end of every working day. If left in the street or gutter, this unwanted material will eventually find its way to the storm drain and ocean.

Reducing Amount of Dust

Establish Footpaths: Keeping construction crews to particular paths, instead of allowing the entire landscape to be trampled upon, will help keep the dust down and prevent a landscape's soil from being compacted and degraded.

Filter Cloth: In windy areas filter cloth may be needed, if not required. Filter cloth is supplied in rolls ranging from two to six feet in width and is staked in place around the perimeter of a property to catch the dust being blown off a property.

Lightly Water the Site: The drier a soil is, the more prone it is to being blown away. Lightly water a site anytime the soil is dry. Water helps create a bond between the soil particles and holds it in place when the wind blows.

PROTECT YOUR EXISTING TOPSOIL

Rich topsoil is not easy to find or make; nor is it cheap to haul in. Because good soil is so important to healthy plants and excellent infiltration, saving whatever amount you have is an ecologically and economically sound idea.

If extensive grading is needed, then move and store as much of this good soil as you can. Keep the stored soil slightly moist, which helps keep the soil's living residents alive. In dry or windy weather, the pile should be lightly watered daily. Either shade or mulch the pile of topsoil if construction is lengthy. Keep the dirtier aspects of construction, like mixing concrete, away from the pile.

GRADING

An ocean friendly garden has contours and curves that meet multiple objectives. Higher areas drain water away from structures, lower water courses move rain water from high places through obstacles that slow and screen runoff, and retention areas capture the runoff. The location and design of this system of moving, slowing and capturing water should already be laid out in the drawings you created in Chapter 2 – and you should use the drawings to efficiently guide you through the grading process. But the location of these elements is only part of the story. To be effective, these undulations will possess certain characteristics.

Depressions: Retention basins and swales work by creating depressions in a landscape. The soil dug out of these depressions should be kept on site; it is probably some of the best soil in the landscape. Sometimes the depressions will take you into the deeper sub-soils, which are nutrient poor. These soils will need to be amended and conditioned before they can support vigorous plants and the goals of infiltration On the other hand, if your design uses a dry creek bed to move rain water into retention areas, rich topsoil is not as important.

Mounds: A mound should be created from soil that is as dense, or is denser, than your existing soil. If imported soil is needed, and it is not as dense as existing, then dig the mound out of your landscape and use the imported soil to fill the area. While dense soil is quicker to produce runoff, it is much less likely to erode and move than more porous soils, such as sandy loam (which is commonly brought into landscapes).

Mounds will settle and erode over time – undermining the contours you are trying to create and making it difficult for the vegetation to successfully root. However, much of this move ment can be avoided by lightly compacting soil as the mound is created. Simply lay down several inches of soil at a time and stomp it into place with your feet – and repeat this process as you build the mound in layers. The larger the mound, the greater the need for compaction.

Perimeter: The soil along the perimeter of a property should be at least one inch lower than the surrounding surface and slope inwards if possible. This small surface depression can make a big difference in the amount of debris-laden runoff your property produces. This practice is especially important in parkways, which should produce no runoff.

RESTORING COMPACTED / DEGRADED SOILS

Compacted soils are common in residential landscapes, the byproduct of too much water, neglect, lack of cover, and/or excessive traffic. Unfortunately, these areas are quick to produce runoff that is laden with sediment and debris.

Naturally, big machines can make a big difference. Roto-tillers and aerators can relatively quickly loosen moist and compacted soils. Or, you can get your exercise for the week by simply digging and turning the soil. But either method is a shortlived remedy if the area is not thoroughly amended and/or planted. Other, greener methods of rejuvenation include:

Let Weeds Grow: The plants capable of growing in compacted soils are unique and well suited to the task of making the area more desirable for other, more favorable plants. If anything, just prevent the weeds from going to seed with a weed whacker or mower.

Water Deep and Infrequently: You can significantly loosen soils through repeating a cycle of watering a site at a very slow rate over a longer length of time (like 5 hours) -- then letting the first 5 inches completely dry before repeating the long slow watering. This type of watering physically moves the soil, creating pore space.

Mulch: Organic matter laid on top or punched into the soil can greatly enhance permeability, as the biological relationship between the two mediums evolves over time. Fine mulches are better for moist areas, whereas heavy mulches are preferable in windy and exposed areas.

Sow Green Manure: There are a variety of plants that are particularly good at improving degraded soils, called green manures. These plants include those that can fixate nitrogen, like clover and vetch, and those that are tough and vigorous, such as alfalfa, millet and rye. These plants are seeded and once they have a hold of landscape they are tilled into the soil and allowed to decompose. The area will be ready for planting 3 months after tilling.

Notes

CHAPTER SEVEN

Irrigation – Laying Pipe

You have successfully designed and drawn a plan for your irrigation system [Chapter 4]. Now is the time to figure out how many trenches you need and where they go. Trenching and rough plumbing is not finish work, and at this point you are only laying the basic structure of the irrigation system: the valve manifold, as well as the main and lateral water supply lines. Finishing the irrigation system, by installing the watering devices, is one of the last steps [Chapter 9].

With the help of this chapter you should be able to determine the amount of irrigation valves needed for your landscape, where the trenches need to be dug, and tips that will make the most of your time and money.

STEPS
Determine amount of valves needed for each hydrozone.
Construct valve assembly
Trench
Lay pipe

THE AMOUNT OF WATERING DEVICES A VALVE CAN HANDLE

A valve is the control that allows you to turn an irrigation line on and off, either manually or automatically. The amount of watering devices you can put on one valve depends on the size of the valve and the amount of water flowing to it.

You already selected the watering devices and determined the proper spacing in the drawing you drafted in Chapter 4. Use the chart below to determine how many devices you can install on one valve. How to put the valves together and connect the valve assembly to the delivery pipes is discussed below.

For the sake of simplicity, the chart below assumes a ¾" valve with the water coming in at 60psi and 160gph (gallons per hour), which is fairly average for a residential landscape.

Overhead Sprinklers *[not recommended when they can be avoided]*

Watering Device	Throw Distance (in feet)	Amount of Heads
Spray Head	8 – 15	7
Rotor Spray Head 1	8 – 15	18
Rotor Spray Head 2	15 – 20	14
Rotor Spray Head 3	30	3
Rotor Spray Head 4	50	1

Low Flow Devices

Watering Device	Delivery Rate	Amount of Heads / Length of Tubing
Emitters	½ gph	125 heads
Misters / Micro-sprayers	1gph	55 heads
Soaker Hose	- - - -	200'
Inline Soaker Tubing	Emitters 12" apart	300'
Inline Soaker Tubing	Emitters 18" apart	400'

1. 1 Valve: 12 heads (18 possible)
2. 1 Valve: 50' of soaker (200' possible)
3. 1 Valve: 35' of soaker (200' possible)
4. 1 Valve: 130' of inline tubing (300' possible)
5. 1 Valve: 145' of inline tubing (300' possible)
6. 1 Valve: 120' of soaker (200' possible)

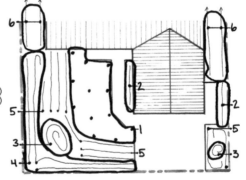

Whenever possible, use the same type of sprinkler heads for each valve, which helps ensure efficient watering.

VALVE ASSEMBLY & DELIVERY PIPES

A valve is a device that allows you to control an irrigation line. You have determined how many valves are necessary for your irrigation system in the plan you drafted in Chapter 4.

If you already have an irrigation system, locate the valve assembly and observe how they were installed to give you a sense of the assembly process. Also compare your existing valve assembly with what your new system will demand, and determine what valves and delivery lines may be re-used in the new system.

Before starting any disassembly of the existing system or construction of the new system, lay out your valve assembly parts on a clean work space (preferably above ground), gather up your tools and materials next to the valve assembly site, and lay out the individual sticks of pipe next to the trenches. When you are ready to begin the work, turn off your main valve supplying water to the house (or if available, a valve supplying only water to the irrigation valve assembly).

IMPORTANT!! Water to the entire house will be disrupted while you are constructing the valve assembly. Be prepared. Try to limit the down time for your family – but don't hurry and do it wrong. Also note that once the valve assembly has been installed and the valve assembly shutoff (#2 on the diagram below) has been closed, water to the house can be turned back on.

Typically, the valves are connected to each other in what is sometimes called a valve assembly or manifold – the series of valves that are all hooked up to a property's main water line. The main lines are the pipes that run from the manifold into trenches and deliver water to the lateral lines and/or directly to the watering devices. Although not tricky or difficult to construct, getting the assembly just right requires experience. If you have a plumber friend, now is the time to ask a favor to help you construct and install the valve system.

Below is an illustration of a valve assembly, but for more detailed illustrations and instructions, visit an irrigation supply or home improvement store.

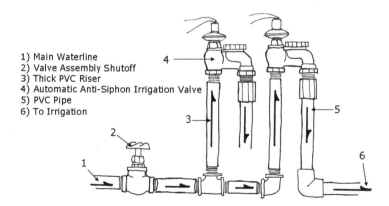

1) Main Waterline
2) Valve Assembly Shutoff
3) Thick PVC Riser
4) Automatic Anti-Siphon Irrigation Valve
5) PVC Pipe
6) To Irrigation

Finally, once the valve assembly is constructed and installed on your main delivery line, you can begin trenching (according to the plan you drew in Chapter 4) and installing the delivery pipes. One method is to start at the valves when roughing in the delivery pipes because the valves won't move once they are installed – but the end point of the delivery line is more flexible. But, do not glue or fasten the pipes coming out of the valves just yet. Simply cut the pieces and temporarily fit them together so that they can move in place while you finish the delivery lines. Next step is to cut and piece together the main and lateral delivery lines in the trenches, When you reach the point where each line will eventually connect with a watering device, install an elbow and a short piece of pipe that will be higher than the ground surface when the trenches are backfilled (the rough "stub up"). For now, drive a stake next to the "stub up" and wire the two together to make sure they stay in place during construction – and tape up the end of the pipe to keep dirt from getting in. The last step in roughing in the irrigation system is to glue each of the joints together – starting from the stub-up and working your way back the valves. Once the system is all glued together, and the glue has dried, you can shovel the dirt back into the trenches, cover the valve assembly with something sturdy to protect it from harm during the continuing construction (like a plastic storage bin), and move on to the next construction phases.

GETTING WATER TO YOUR HYDROZONES
Trenching and Laying Pipe
From a trenching perspective, soaker hose and inline tubing require the least amount of digging. Overhead sprinklers, on the other hand, can be trench intensive. An irrigation line is comprised of a main line, lateral lines, and the watering devices.

The illustration below shows how the trenches would look for the valves determined in the illustration. Refer to the "layer drawing" from chapter 4 for hydrozone location.

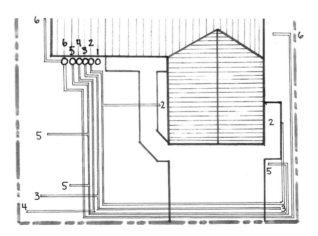

The illustration above shows the main lines for the 5 low flow valves (#1 is a spare valve for possible future additions). Although it looks like a lot of work, most of the pipes share trenches and digging for this irrigation system would go fairly quickly.

TIPS
Re-Use Old PVC: Irrigation systems are commonly dug up during landscape renovation, and the

PVC pipe pulled out can be used again for the new main and lateral lines. Manufacturing PVC pipe is notoriously harmful to the environment, and not only will you be reducing these environmental costs, but saving yourself money. Note: PVC gets brittle as it ages and is less likely to bend. Make sure the PVC pipe you re-use is in good condition and does not leak or break.

Share Trenches: Wherever possible, the main and lateral lines should share the same trench. Trenching can be damaging to soil ecology and excessive trenching can be harmful to a landscape's health. Sharing trenches will also save you a lot of time.

Don't Make the Trenches Too Deep: Unless you experience a freeze every winter, irrigation pipes do not always have to be deep. A deep pipe drives up maintenance costs, which in turn reduces an irrigation system's adaptability. Irrigation pipes under concrete and walkways, or in areas where shovels are commonly used, like annual and perennial beds, should be deep. Pipes along walls, and in beds with large shrubs and trees should be only a couple of inches deep; too deep and roots will grow over the pipes.

An Ounce of Prevention is Worth a Pound of Cure! Make sure that the underground plumbing is made of durable materials and is installed properly. Avoid bending the pipe to fit pieces together, or any other stress on the fittings – the plumbing should go together easily and lie in place without forcing it. Also, carefully follow the instructions for joining pipes and fittings. A leak or break in the underground plumbing will require digging up your garden and often dirty and difficult repairs – a fate worth carefully avoiding in the first place.

Notes

CHAPTER **8** EIGHT

Permeability

*Although hardscape, such as walkways, patios and driveways,
is normally thought of as being impermeable, it can be designed to be
permeable; that is, made of materials and/or designs that allow water
to be absorbed. In contrast, impermeable surfaces are made from
materials intended to keep the underlying area dry (the most
important example being your roof).*

Increasing the amount of permeable surfaces in appropriate places is both an economically and ecologically important component of an Ocean Friendly Garden. Permeable surfaces slow down water -- eliminating fast moving "sheets" of water -- which allows sediment and other pollutants to drop out before reaching the street and storm drain. These surfaces also spread the process of water infiltration over a greater area, not relying wholly on retention areas (discussed in Chapter 10). In fact, permeable surfaces can infiltrate as much as 70% to 80% of annual rainfall that would otherwise run off your property. Permeable surfaces can also be less expensive than impermeable concrete or asphalt.

STEPS
Identify opportunities for permeable surfaces
Select material
Prepare the area

CHANGING SURFACES
Every year about 27,000 gallons of rainwater runs off the average residential landscape in Huntington Beach (CA). Considering that the average was calculated from a sample of 36,000 home-sites, that's an amazing amount of water flowing into the Pacific Ocean.

The reason the average landscape sheds so much water is due to its composition: Of the total landscape (which includes the house, roof, driveways, patios, and garden areas) only 40% of it is typically permeable. But there are opportunities to eliminate much of the impermeable surface area in our landscape. Unlike areas that need to remain dry for safety reasons, like porches at entryways; walkways, patios and even driveways can be designed to allow infiltration and eliminate runoff.

Huntington Beach is not unlike a lot of urban communities. In fact, all of us can do a much better job at reducing residential runoff. Below are the many options that can be employed to create a landscape and garden that is as good for you as it is for the ocean.

Driveways

Driveways are notorious pollution "hot spots" due to oil leaks, brake dust, and other pollutants falling from our cars. These pollutants wash off driveways and into the ocean when we clean our cars, hose off tools, and wage the occasional but inevitable water fight. Driveways also occupy a lot of space, so they are the source of a large volume of runoff during rain events. Therefore, retaining or screening the water that runs off driveways is a big part of creating an Ocean Friendly Garden. While almost all concrete and asphalt driveways can be replaced with pavers, not all driveways warrant the expense.

You should decide whether it makes more sense to capture and divert the runoff into your garden or if it's better to tear up and replace an existing driveway. While replacing an existing driveway may add expense, it also adds an opportunity to incorporate the new driveway materials in the design and beauty of your landscape.

Safety is the rule when choosing permeable surfaces. The more an area is used, the safer it should be. And generally, the more stable and safe a surface is, the less permeable it tends to be. A driveway must provide a safe point of entry for your family and your visitors. Many driveways are configured in such a way that safety and high permeability can work in concert. Below are some of the materials and ideas for driveways.

Brick and Pavers: These building materials are semi-permeable and provide a relatively safe surface. One of the benefits of brick and pavers is low cost. Requiring no special equipment, the average homeowner can install a driveway.

Brick and pavers can also be installed in strips cut into your existing driveway – lowering the work and expense while providing a more attractive driveway that captures some of the runoff.

Gravel: Although certainly not trendy, easy to walk on, nor practical on slopes of any kind, nothing beats gravel for permeability and ease of installation. Gravel also supports a more biologically diverse landscape.

In some cases, a simple gravel strip in the center of the driveway will be very effective at capturing the water and pollutants, while not interfering with safety or requiring much maintenance.

Turf Blocks: Coming in a variety of forms, turf blocks provide a surface cars can drive on, while providing gaps that ground covers can grow in. This green alternative is highly permeable. Unless the area is large, turf is not recommended as the ground cover because of the maintenance costs. Refer to the list on www.surfrider.org/ofg

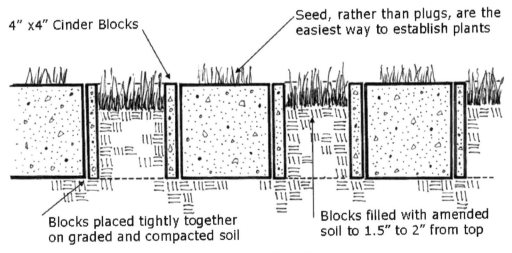

4" x4" Cinder Blocks

Seed, rather than plugs, are the easiest way to establish plants

Blocks placed tightly together on graded and compacted soil

Blocks filled with amended soil to 1.5" to 2" from top

Cross Section: Turf Blocks

Stone: Breaking up a driveway with stone is an attractive alternative to turf blocks and pavers. In some cases, such as the one pictured below, a stone strip can help lead sheeting water to retention areas, much like a grate.

Grates: A drainage grate or "channel drain", is a low-cost option which produces excellent results. Grates are cut into driveways to divert sheeting water. The runoff is captured by the grate, connected sub-surface pipe and then guided to screening, cleaning and retention devices.

Grates are recommended on sloped driveways.

Even simple changes to a driveway can influence the direction of a lot of water. The drainage-grate set into the driveway in this picture directs roof, patio, and driveway run-off into the garden, diverting about 10,000 gallons of water per year from flowing into the ocean.

DRIVEWAYS AND OIL

Oil running off driveways, collecting debris and particulates as it makes its way to the storm drain system and ocean, is an all-too-common problem in urban communities. Even the most immaculate and well-maintained cars can sometimes leak fluids.

Many of the fluids used in automobiles are long lasting and resistant to degradation. The goal is to either prevent water running across areas with oil, or to direct the water with oil in it to the landscape. These are some of the strategies to manage fluids from cars:

- Create a permeable area under the parked cars, called an oil strip. This area can be planted, filled with gravel, or filled with loosely fitted brick and pavers.
- Direct the water sheeting down a driveway to the garden, where the oil and particulates can be filtered out. Installing a drainage grate beyond the parked cars is the easiest and least expensive method for diverting driveway runoff.
- Protect the storm drains from oil-laden runoff with fiber rolls, mini-gabions, and vegetation such as perennial grasses on the perimeter of your property
- Prior to your rainy season, or on a regular basis, use absorbent materials to clean up the oil before the rain starts. Then safely dispose of the oil-laden materials. Auto mechanics and auto part stores can help identify home remedies and store-bought materials.
- If the parking area is regularly used by cars that leak oil, as at apartment complexes, then cover the parking stalls with an impermeable surface, such as plywood or fiberglass sheets. These coverings will prevent rain from falling directly on the oily areas.
- Cars that leak excessively are illegal and the owner can be issued a citation. Leaking cars are illegal on both public and private land. Fix your leaks and help your neighbors do the same – we'll all benefit from being good neighbors.

Paths & Patios

Just as you did in the Planning Chapters 2, 3 and 4, divide your paths and patios into three areas: those with high, medium, or low use. The higher the use; the denser the material needed. Below are recommendations for these three areas of use, with the description of the materials further on.

High Use: bricks and pavers

Medium Use: brick, pavers, decomposed granite, tightly placed stone

Low Use: decomposed granite, stone, pea gravel, and mulch

Keeping some concrete can be beneficial. Concrete can provide a clean transition from the garden to the house, and helps keep the dust, dirt, bugs, and moisture from getting into the house.

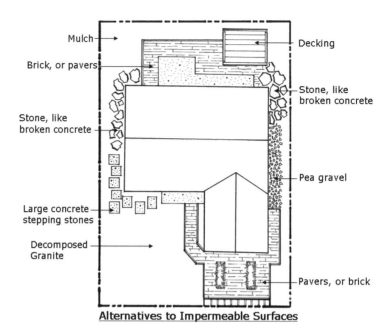

Alternatives to Impermeable Surfaces

COMPARING MATERIALS

Selecting materials is a negotiation between safety and ease of use, aesthetics, degree of permeability, and installation / maintenance costs. The chart below will help you select the ideal surface for your situation.

The more textured and rougher the material, the better; roughness provides friction, which in turn slows water, allowing some of the debris to settle out. All the materials listed below work best on grades of 6% or less.

Surface	Costs	Infiltration	Good Uses & Notes
Brick	*Moderate to high installation costs; low to moderate maintenance costs.*	*Low to high, depending on size of gaps.*	*Tight (closely spaced) brick can be used for all residential needs; loose brick, those with wider spaces, are good for infrequently used walkways.*
Crushed Aggregate	*Low maintenance and installation costs. Weeds can become a problem.*	*High.*	*Crushed aggregate is a common, all-purpose surface, but is not common in urban communities; tough on bare feet and children and is not considered attractive. Pea gravel is better on feet, but is not as porous as crushed aggregate.*

Surface	Costs	Infiltration	Good Uses & Notes
Decking	High installation and maintenance costs. Should budget for replacing it every 15 years. However, wood is a renewable resource that pulls CO2 from the atmosphere, unlike pavers, brick and concrete. A newly available product is planks and railing material made from recycled plastic – extremely durable and one way to keep plastics out of our landfills (and ocean).	Moderate to high, depending on gaps between planks and the surface below the deck.	While expensive to install, decks can provide a wonderful retreat in a garden; they can elevate, encapsulate, and captivate a visitor.
Decomposed Granite	Low installation costs, but more expensive than similar materials, like pea gravel and mulches. Low maintenance costs.	Moderate to high.	Excellent for garden paths and away from house entrances. It sticks to the bottom of shoes.
Pavers	Moderate installation and low maintenance costs.	Low to high, depending on gaps and degree of slope.	Easily installed and repaired, pavers come in a wide variety of shapes, sizes, and colors, and because of their aesthetic versatility, are being used with growing frequency.
Porous Asphalt	High installation and low maintenance costs.	Low to moderate.	Good replacement for current asphalt driveways. However, it is petroleum based and produces dirty run-off.
Porous Concrete	High installation and low maintenance costs.	Low to moderate.	Can be used instead of conventional concrete anywhere around a home.
Stone – Natural, Recycled, or Manufactured	Low to high installation costs, depending on the type of stone. Low to moderate maintenance costs, depending on the types of plants and materials used to fill the gaps.	Moderate to high, depending on size and spacing.	Excellent for paths and patios. Not all stone has to be laid in sand, but can be sunken into the soil instead, where plants are grown around them.

Surface	Costs	Infiltration	Good Uses & Notes
Turf Block	*Moderate installation costs and moderate to high maintenance costs (if the grass has to be mowed and regularly irrigated).*	*Moderate to high.*	*Great for short term parking areas. Tough to properly irrigate if cars are always on it. There are low maintenance plants that can be used with these blocks.*
MULCHES			
Bark	*Low installation and maintenance costs.*	*High.*	*Fine bark is good for walking surfaces, and large bark for holding soil in windy, exposed areas.*
Gorilla Hair	*Moderately expensive for mulches; low maintenance costs.*	*High.*	*Provides a comfy walking surface, unlike other mulches. Made from long, thin shavings of redwood or cedar.*
Rock	*Expensive for mulches; low maintenance costs.*	*Moderate to high, depending on spaces between rocks and surface below.*	*River rock is not a good walking surface, but perfect for windy, exposed areas. Excellent mulch for tough Mediterranean plants.*
Tree Shredding	*If not free, then low installation costs; low maintenance costs.*	*High.*	*Great for weed control. Will divert some of the available nitrogen in soil, and plants may show signs of deficiency.*

CONSTRUCTING PERMEABLE SURFACES

Below are the steps and materials needed to lay your permeable surface.

Barrier Cloth: Lying below the base material, barrier cloth has one or two functions. This cloth can prevent weeds from coming up from below the base material, reducing maintenance costs. The cloth can also be used to separate materials, such as gravel and dirt, preventing the heavier materials from blending and sinking into the underlying soil. Barrier cloth is used under decomposed granite, brick, pavers, and gravel, but not mulches, where it is fairly short lived.

Base Material: Increasing permeability not only implies changing the ground surfaces, but the materials under the ground surface too. Base material lies under porous concrete, brick and pavers. Base material is usually gravel and/or sand. Crushed stone is best because it has the highest amount of pore space (35% to 40%). Base material should not include fine materials, such as pea gravel and the finest sand, because of the reduced pore space.

Dirt: Turf blocks and stone are commonly laid in the existing soil, in order to support the plants going in around them. Turf blocks are simply laid over a graded surface, then backfilled and seeded. Stones need to be set, rather than laid. Lightly tilled dirt is built up and stones are set one at a time by completely saturating the area under the stone and floating it until it is at the proper height and angle.

Grading: Good grading will lead water away from a house and into a garden. Nothing less than a 2% grade (slope) is required for driveways, paths and patios. 2% means a two inch drop for every ten foot run. Guidelines help ensure the proper grade. Made from strong string or lumber, guidelines are typically set every five feet and represent the finished grade.

Compaction: Everything settles, even concrete. The degree that your project settles is up to you. Compaction is the key in preventing settling. Mechanical vibrating compactors are perfect for large, sandy areas. Rollers (barrels of water drawn over an area) are ideal for smaller areas. Thoroughly soaking a site, and allowing it to dry, will also help soil settle. Mechanical compacters and rollers are readily available to rent.

TIPS

Pipes: Do not forget to lay a couple of extra pipes under driveways, paths and patios – you'll never know when you'll need them. Changes in irrigation or lighting can create a sudden need for more pipes than originally planned for. Just lay a couple of PVC pipes in the ground and cover the ends with duct tape before covering the area and constructing your driveway, patio or pathways. The added expense of installing them now is minimal, and much less than tearing up the area later. Mark the location of your pipes on your landscape plan.

Timing: Take your time to prepare and grade an area for permeable surfaces. Lack of foresight and proper preparation will lead to unsafe surfaces and/or unwanted drainage problems. Once the final grade is finished, quickly lay down the final surface, before the grade is disturbed.

Peaks and Valleys: Intentionally created with bricks and pavers, peaks and valleys help move or trap water. Peaks are used in driveways and patios to stop water from pooling. Valleys are used in parkways, where runoff should be trapped and held.

Notes

CHAPTER NINE

Irrigation – Attaching Watering Devices

Second only to planning, this is the step that most influences an irrigation system's efficiency – proper assembly ensures no leaks; completely flushing the pipes ensures the heads perform to specification; and properly programming the irrigation controller to match the needs of your hydrozones will help sustain a beautiful landscape without wasting water.

With your grading completed and the main and lateral lines already in the ground, it is time to finish building the irrigation system.

STEPS
Flush system

Put on watering devices

Test and tune (several times)

Install controller

Determine Valve Run Times

FLUSH SYSTEM

After gluing the main and lateral lines, and burying the pipes, dirt and debris has probably gotten into the pipes. Removing that debris from pipes is critical. Sprinkler heads, drip irrigation, and inline soaker tubing will never work right if debris is clogging these watering devices. To ensure the system works properly for a long time, you need to flush out the pipes at the beginning, and then ensure no debris gets back in the system.

Start by clearing away the soil around the end of each delivery line. Next, install the connector fitting onto the watering device and hold it along side of the stub-up – measure and mark where the pipe needs to be cut to ensure the device is above ground, but doesn't stick up too high. Remove the connector from the device, cut the stub-up to the proper height, carefully clean off the ragged edges with sand paper, and glue the connector to the stub-up. Repeat this process with each stub-up.

Flushing a system involves turning on a value and letting the water gush until it is absolutely clear. The sprinkler heads, drip tubing and heads, and soaker lines are installed immediately after flushing. Do each valve individually – flushing and finishing the installation of the watering devices on that valve before flushing out the system on the next valve. Flushing the system one valve at a time will help keep dirt from getting back in the pipes during the construction.

It is also important to stop the debris-laden water from flooding back into the pipes once the water is turned off. To avoid this, you will have to channel the flooding water away from the stub-ups.

INSTALL the WATER DEVICES, TEST & TUNE

Each watering device is a little different, and the order of assembling the parts will differ. For example, sprinkler heads often require lateral lines from the main line and once each sprinkler head is installed, you're done. By comparison, a drip system may require first installing the distribution head, then cutting the tubing to the location of each drip device, then installing the individual spray heads. The best installation of a soaker line may be to install an "L" (a 90 degree turn) before the connector so that the soaker lies flat on the ground. Before beginning any of the construction, it is always best to open the packages, read the instructions, and familiarize yourself with the parts and the order of the steps to final installation. Understanding all the steps beforehand will help avoid mistakes at the beginning.

Finally, you should manually turn on the individual valves to test and tune up the system. Make sure that each device is functioning properly and that there aren't any leaks. It is best to test and observe the system several times, because it may take a few times to fully fill the system with water and reach the pressure you can expect in the future.

IRRIGATION CONTROLLERS
Weather-Based Timers

A weather-based timer will calculate your landscape's water needs according to the weather, and turn on the valves individually to meet the demands of each hydrozone. The timer does this by taking the information you give it about your landscape and combining that with information it gets from the nearest weather station. It calculates the amount of water needed by determining the amount of water being used by your plants.

Weather-based timers are the most efficient irrigation controller for established landscapes, large lots, and gardens close to a weather station. The timer is a little unyielding for gardens that change a lot, and those where the weather station is in a different microclimate. In most situations, once it is properly programmed, a weather-based timer should be efficient – as well as maintenance and worry free.

CONVENTIONAL IRRIGATION CONTROLLERS

For all the conveniences of conventional irrigation controllers, they tend to over water -- and inattentiveness is the primary reason. At the very least, watering schedules should be adjusted at least once a month. Unfortunately, it's not uncommon to find that conventional timers are only adjusted four times a year, or less often. A common misperception is that you can't over water your plants. The truth is, your garden will suffer from over watering and the waste will likely just carry off more pollutants to the ocean.

Below are some tips that should help you adjust your timer more frequently.

Accessible: Put the timer where it is super easy to get at, and in a well lit place where you frequently visit. A good place for a conventional timer is in the garage, next to the switches that turn on the garage's lights.

Get to Know Them: Programming irrigation controllers is easy. Really! They have the same sort of logic that cell phones have, a simple list of menus and methods to scroll through. With a little patience and attention to the instructions, it will take you no more than 30 minutes to program and understand your timer.

Seasonal Adjustment: A feature rarely used on irrigation controllers (despite the fact that most have them) is the seasonal adjuster. This feature allows you to turn the entire irrigation system up or down by percentages, instead of reprogramming each station. These adjustments are handy when unusual weather happens, such as summer fog and moisture.

Accessories: Rain and soil moisture sensors are two controller accessories that can save a lot of water and allow your plants to thrive. The rain sensor will shut the system down when it rains. And the soil moisture sensor will only allow a valve to be activated once soil moisture hits a certain point – matching the demands of your plants.

DETERMINING VALVE RUN TIMES

Programming a timer sounds easy. All you have to do is tell the timer when to turn a valve on, how long it should run, and how frequent it should run. The catch, however, is determining the duration (how long) and frequency. Determining watering times means juggling six influences: the type of watering device, type of soil, the type and size of plants, the time of year, and your location.

Luckily, there are a variety of water calculators available online that will help you develop a watering schedule for your unique landscape. Water districts commonly provide water calculators on their websites.

As a general rule: the quicker the water delivery, the shorter the duration and frequency. Below are the watering times for our example landscape.

Plant Type	Watering Device	Summer	Spring and Fall	Winter
Turf	Rotor Spray Heads	8 minutes every 2 days	7 minutes every 3 days	off / 8 minutes every 6 days
Ground Covers	Rotor Spray Heads	10 minutes every 3 days	10 minutes every 5 days	off
Perennials	Soaker Hose	25 minutes every 3 days	20 minutes every 4 days	off
Shrubs	Inline Emitter Tubing	3 hours every 4 days	2.5 hours every 7 days	off
Trees	Inline Soaker Tubing	6 hours every 7 days	5 hours every 10 days	off

TIPS

Swing Joints: Sprinkler heads and hoses attached to PVC are prone to being kicked or run over. A small geyser of wasted water and a lengthy repair job ensues. To reduce the chances of damage when kicked, put swing joints on all pipes leading to the surface (your stub-up). A swing joint is two threaded "L"s screwed together, providing a wide range of motion.

Mulch: PVC, poly tubing and plastic watering devices are solar sensitive and will eventually degrade in the sun. Exposed irrigation components should be lightly covered with a ½" layer of mulch. Protecting irrigation system components is an ongoing task.

Test and Tune Regularly: Filters fill, heads clog, and hoses move about - irrigation systems are hardly static. Regular maintenance is needed for optimum performance. Checking each valve once a month will help keep maintenance costs low and performance high.

Secret Misbehavior: Many cities recommend, if not demand, that we water in the pre-dawn hours. This practice reduces water lost to evaporation and can save your plants from getting scorched. The down side is that we rarely see the irrigation system operating, and we can go long periods of time before witnessing broken, leaky or misplaced irrigation devices. We waste water and our garden suffers. So, occasionally turn on each valve manually and walk around to inspect for leaks and other problems with the watering devices.

CHAPTER TEN

Retention

Re-designing our landscaped areas to retain water mimics natural processes that once occurred before we paved and developed our watersheds. The outcome of retaining water on our property will result in a beautiful and more self-sustaining garden, as well as realizing benefits to our community, our local waterways and the ocean. Retention/infiltration areas not only remove debris and pollutants, but can help recharge a local aquifer, increasing local water supplies.

In this chapter you will find descriptions of various devices that can be easily constructed to retain water, providing an opportunity for infiltration. However, there are communities, areas, and landscapes that can ill afford to load up the land with water. These areas may be prone to landslides, or sit above areas known for erosion. If soil slips or erosion are a concern, then call a professional. See Chapter 12 for more information on determining if your landscape is safe and appropriate for retaining water on-site.

Screening and cleaning runoff are strategies for people that can not retain water on their property. These strategies and tools can also be incorporated into a design that captures most any rain event, but also anticipates extraordinary rains that the retention devices cannot catch. Screening is relatively easy and involves removing debris from runoff. Cleaning relies on biological processes to extract pollutants, such as pathogens, metals and nutrients. These tools are discussed in Chapter 11.

STEPS
Select and install retention devices

INFILTRATION DEVICES

An infiltration area is anywhere water is directed and allowed to sit and slowly percolate into the ground. There are two types of infiltration areas, those above ground and those below. Above ground means that water is visible and includes devices such as infiltration basins, dry creek beds, seasonal ponds, and swales. Below ground devices include dry wells and infiltration trenches.

Above ground infiltration devices are preferred over underground. The water sitting in above ground devices can be easily monitored; the sediment that accumulates can be effortlessly removed; and installation and maintenance costs are much lower. On the other hand, below ground devices are used when space is limited and can be built under porous walkways, planter beds, and even parking lots.

Importantly, even our best efforts to capture, retain and infiltrate all the rain water from unusually large rain events can fail. Having an exit strategy for this excessive water will greatly reduce the ill-effects during a large storm. Always give the runoff a safe exit from your landscape.

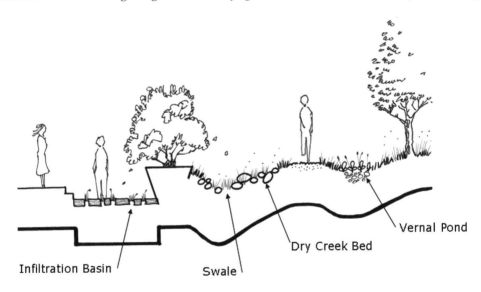

Vernal Pond

Dry Creek Bed

Infiltration Basin

Swale

Above Ground Retention Devices

ABOVE GROUND INFILTRATION DEVICES

Dry Creek Bed: A dry creek bed is dug into a garden and filled with rock. They are an attractive, effective way to handle runoff. Raking and sweeping dry creeks can be difficult though. Swales are often a better option for areas with frequent runoff, because they are easier to clean and maintain. The main difference between dry creek beds and swales is that the former is not designed to encourage plant growth. But, both a dry creek bed and a swale can provide a pathway for rain water to an infiltration basin or seasonal pond.

Infiltration Basins: An infiltration basin is a place where water is allowed to accumulate to mini-pond-like conditions. As the photos above and below show, these areas can be conspicuous, or not; one looks like an infiltration area, and the other just a sunken patio. Plants are recommended for infiltration basins; they ensure infiltration and aid in screening/cleaning. Wherever possible, infiltration basins should be lower in elevation than the foundation of your house.

Importantly, a retention basin should be located in an area that allows the water to infiltrate deep into the soils. For instructions on how to determine the types of soil in your garden – see Chapter 4. Also, see the Tips in this chapter for a simple "percolation test."

If you discover that an infiltration area does not drain within three days after a normal rain event, then it should either be redesigned and reconstructed, or moved to a more favorable spot.

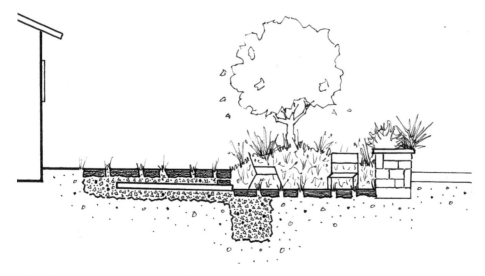

This illustration is a cross section of the picture above and shows how runoff is directed and trapped. An infiltration trench leads the water to the infiltration basin, where a dry well aids in percolation.

Although not large, this basin helps clean and move hundreds of gallons of runoff.

Swales: A swale is used to both channel water and allow infiltration. Often referred to as bio-swales, all swales are planted, which helps to stabilize the swale shoulders against erosion and slippage, and slows and filters runoff. Swales are preferred over dry creek beds in areas that get regular use, because they are easier to clean and maintain. The sediment collected from swales will be high in nutrients and can be used throughout a garden. Perennial grasses and riparian plants are recommended for swales because of their aggressive roots and tolerance for wet/dry conditions.

Running through the middle of the landscape, this swale handles thousands of gallons of runoff a year.

Vernal / Seasonal Ponds: A rarity in urban environments, and borrowed from the native ones, a vernal pond is an infiltration area planted with plants that can survive on rainfall and runoff alone. These depressions are not irrigated. Vernal ponds are ideally suited for large properties, and are used to capture and temporarily store a lot of water.

Below Ground Infiltration Devices

If a below ground device is fed with runoff from the surface, then the water will have to be thoroughly screened before entering. Even the smallest particles will eventually fill a device, causing failure.

Dry Well: Mostly below ground, a dry well is a large pit lined with filter fabric and filled with a variety of porous objects. Aggregate, milk crates, and plastic boxes are commonly used. Dry wells are generally no smaller than 3' by 3' by 3', and in most situations, much larger. An inspection port, which is a three to four inch pipe used to monitor water levels, is typical on large wells (refer to the illustration below). Like the infiltration trench described next, dry wells will lose efficiency over time.

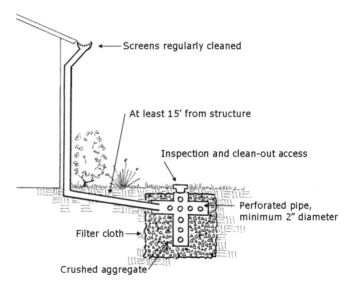

Removing particles before the runoff fills the dry well is essential in creating an efficient device. As the aggregate fills with sediment, the rate of infiltration slows, and only digging up and cleaning the gravel will restore efficiency. These devices work best in sandy soils.

Screens regularly cleaned

At least 15' from structure

Inspection and clean-out access

Perforated pipe, minimum 2" diameter

Filter cloth

Crushed aggregate

Dry Well Connected to Downspout

Infiltration Trench: These are trenches dug into the ground and filled with an aggregate like gravel. An infiltration trench can be above or below ground.

Once the trench is dug, it is lined in filter cloth which will wrap around the gravel that is poured into the trench. There are a variety of uses for these easily constructed devices: they can be used around a home to divert water away from the foundation (called French drains); they can be used to guide roof water falling from the eaves or exiting a rain gutter's downspout; and they can be used along the edge of a property, providing the last defense against runoff. An infiltration trench will become ineffective over time, as small particles either fill the pores in the

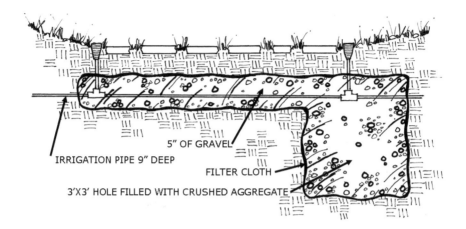

IRRIGATION PIPE 9" DEEP

5" OF GRAVEL

FILTER CLOTH

3'X3' HOLE FILLED WITH CRUSHED AGGREGATE

filter cloth, or fill the gaps in the gravel. Depending on your weather conditions and the soil in your landscape, infiltration trenches will need to be cleaned every three to ten years to maintain maximum efficiency.

TIPS

Know Your Soil: Before you design an infiltration device for your landscape, test your soil. Dig a two cubic foot hole and fill it half full with water. If the water is still visible after 72 hours, then the site is not suitable for an infiltration device.

Take Your Best Shot: It is difficult to exactly calculate the space and capacity of your landscape required to capture and infiltrate the water from any rain event. Instead, estimate your landscape's runoff in an average rain event (see the formula at the end of Chapter 2) and estimate the area needed to catch the water – including the creation of more permeable surfaces, the dry creek beds and swales, the retention/infiltration areas, and finally the trenches. Obviously, the more space the better.

CHAPTER ELEVEN

Screening and Cleaning Runoff

Some landscapes can not retain and infiltrate rain water.
Maybe the size of the garden area is not sufficient to
capture the volume of water from the impervious surfaces
in your landscape. Or the slope of your landscape
is too steep to safely capture and retain
runoff. In these situations screening and/or
cleaning runoff becomes the priority.

Screening means removing debris from the runoff. The size of the debris removed depends on the type of device used. Cleaning means removing water borne (soluble) pollutants, such as nutrients, pathogens, and metals. Cleaning devices rely on biological processes. Often, the same constituents in the water that are so harmful to the ocean are actually beneficial to a healthy garden.

STEPS
Select and install device

SCREENING RUNOFF
The devices and techniques are listed in alphabetical order. Some of these devices are small and perfect for small areas. Others are typically used at the entrance to a storm drain that may or may not be right for your property. The list is an attempt to give you a comprehensive array of alternatives for cleaning and screening runoff – both on-site and off. You will have to select the device that is appropriate for your circumstances.

Barriers Around Drains: You can protect the ocean by protecting the storm drains that lead to it. Luckily, there are a lot of materials and devices that can be employed. Some of the many materials are:

Fiber Roles: Made from straw, rice hulls, and even coconut waste, these organic rolls circle a drain, ensuring that any water that gets to the drain passes through the roll. Slightly dug into the ground, fiber rolls should be staked if the flow of water is either voluminous or fast. Fiber rolls will need to be replaced every year, as they quickly break down and begin contributing their own debris.

Filter Cloth: Typically a nylon fabric, there are many types of filter fabric. There are cloths that filter silt, sediment, wind, soil, and water. If the cloth is going under ground, then spend the money to buy quality; replacing cloth is expensive.

Trenches: Protect a storm drain with a trench full of gravel – quick and effective. The liner between the soil and aggregate does not have to be permeable.

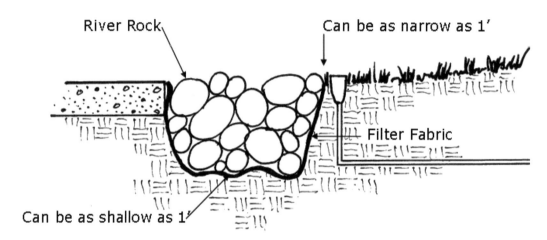

Last Defense Trench

Mini-Gabion: Although not widely used, mini-gabions are used like fiber rolls, but are longer lasting and more effective. These devices are made by wrapping a large aggregate, like broken concrete, in chicken wire. They can be almost any size and length. If partially buried, as commonly done, then the soil side will need to be protected with filter cloth.

Planting: Plants hold their ground, and a lot of the ground that tries to pass them. Planting around a storm drain can slow and filter incoming runoff. The plants around storm drains are selected because of their ability to thrive without fertilizers and pesticides.

Riprap: Guarding the perimeter of a storm drain, piles of large rock can slow run-off and catch the larger debris. Riprap is recommended for areas with fast moving water. It can be almost any size and include broken concrete.

Catch Basins: Looking like a large concrete box, catch basins are dug into the ground and are used to catch debris. Catch basins are commonly used when space is limited and the water moves fairly fast. These devices will catch sediment if the water slows.

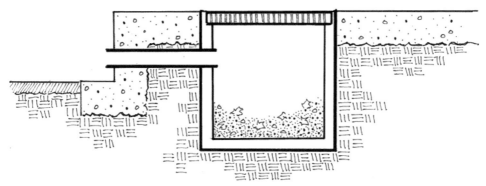

Mechanical Catch Basin

Drainage Grate/Channel Drain: Drainage grates are typically a "bar rack" that covers a trough – which collects water and debris and diverts it to the garden before it can reach the street. These grated troughs work best when installed along the perimeters of driveways, often a source of runoff leaving the property that is otherwise difficult to capture and divert.
Sediment Traps: A sediment trap or small pond is a widening in a channel that allows runoff to slow and drop its heavier particles. Sediment traps are part of a drainage system, such as swales. Sediment traps can be permeable, or not; and planted, or not. If effective, sediment traps will need regular cleaning.

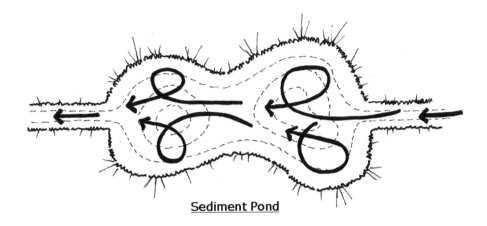

Sediment Pond

CLEANING RUNOFF

Bio-Catch Basin: Much like a standard catch basin, a biological catch basin is primarily used to screen debris. However, when the flow of runoff is not great, a bio-catch basin can also remove nutrients and pathogens from runoff.

Biological Catch Basin

Constructed Wetlands: A constructed wetland is a depression where runoff is allowed to slowly pass through your landscape. They may be perpetually wet or moist. Typically the lowest point in a landscape, wetlands do not have to be permeable. Particles are removed from runoff through filtering and sedimentation. Because of the plants and biologically active soil, wetlands can also remove nutrients, metals, and pathogens. Constructed wetlands will need to be cleaned every three to five years.

TIPS

Clean: Screening devices need to be cleaned at least once a year, before the start of rain. If a rain event is large, or your season long, then the screening devices will need more frequent clean-

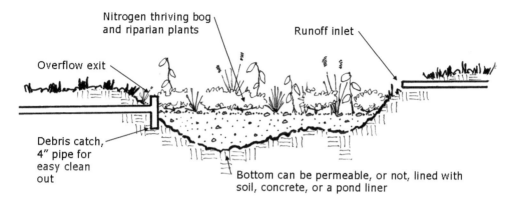

Nitrogen thriving bog
and riparian plants

Runoff inlet

Overflow exit

Debris catch,
4" pipe for
easy clean
out

Bottom can be permeable, or not, lined with
soil, concrete, or a pond liner

Constructed Wetlands

ing. The stuff that comes out of screening and cleaning devices is excellent for a garden. Either throw it into a compost pile, or use it as a fertilizer and soil amendment throughout your landscape.

Have Fortitude: The use of cleaning devices is not for the faint of heart. The small ecosystem you created to remove pollutants will eventually fill with sediment and need to be thoroughly cleaned, which may involve pulling out the plants and removing several inches of soil, all of which completely disrupts the organisms that inhabit the site.

Summer Water: The type of plants capable of pulling nutrients and metals from runoff are naturally found along streams. While many of these plants are drought adapted, most would prefer moist soil. Summer watering is recommended to keep these plants healthy, and prepared for the rainy season.

Notes

Hillsides and Slopes

Managing a slope is tricky, and sometimes even risky. Wind, water, and gravity have greater impacts on slopes, and naturally, the greater the degree of slope, the greater the impact.

CPR has three goals for slopes: Protect a hillside against soil slips and topsoil loss; Encourage water infiltration wherever it's safe; and Screen the water that does leave.

Understanding your degree of erosion risk is the first step in reaching the three goals. This chapter provides information to help you identify the risky portions of your slopes. Areas that can handle infiltration and screening devices are then identified. Lastly, this chapter will help you select devices that will help you stabilize your hillside.

STEPS
Know when to call a professional
Determine likelihood of topsoil loss
Determine most appropriate methods for control
Use tips for greatest efficiency

KNOW YOUR TERRIAN
Surveying your property is the first step in creating a landscape that works for you and the ocean. Your survey will identify areas prone to runoff, places for infiltration, and the best locations for screening runoff.

Identifying Risky Areas
Erosion is the separation and transportation of soil particles. Erosion includes topsoil loss, landslides, and soil slips. Topsoil loss is much different from soil slips and landslides. Topsoil loss occurs within the first couple inches of a landscape. Landslides and soil slips are mass

movements of mud and rock, and usually occur suddenly. Naturally, the likelihood of all types of erosion increases with the amount of water falling on or coming into a landscape.

If you suspect that your landscape or an adjoining neighbor's property may be prone to landslides or soil slips, then do not hold water on your property and call a registered geo-technical engineer for recommendations.

Erosion / Top-Soil Loss Test

It is possible to estimate the chance of water runoff and topsoil loss by evaluating four factors: The steepness of a slope, the type of vegetation, the site's type of soil, and the amount of activity by animals and humans. Below is a simple test that can be used to evaluate these four factors on your property. The test allows you to score your property for the four conditions, and add up the scores to estimate your risk of erosion.

The erosion test below provides indicators to the likelihood of erosion, but cannot give accurate data. If you need accurate data for erosion risk, consult a local Certified Professional Soil Erosion and Sediment Control Specialist (CPESC). This test was adapted from Universal Soil Loss Equation, a nationwide standard developed for farmers.

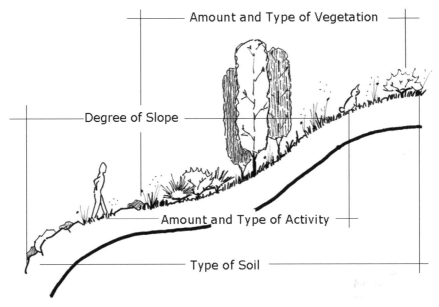

Slope

The incline and length of a slope are two measurable factors that most affect the chances of runoff and topsoil loss. As a general rule, when the slope's degree and length double, the chances of erosion also double. For example, a 100-foot slope has twice the erosion likelihood of a 50-foot slope and a 40 degree slope has double the risk of erosion compared to a 20 degree slope.

Steepness of Slope

0–16%	1 point
17–34%	2 points
35–51%	4 points
52% and higher	8 points

Length of Slope

0–25 feet	1 point
26–50 feet	2 points
51–100 feet	4 points
101–200 feet	8 points

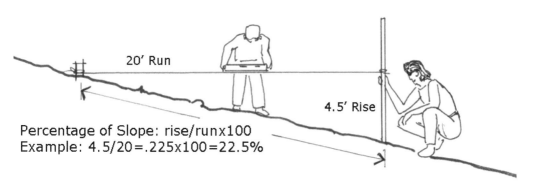

20' Run

4.5' Rise

Percentage of Slope: rise/runx100
Example: 4.5/20=.225x100=22.5%

Type and Density of Plants

This gauge is a forest-versus-bare soil comparison. Not surprisingly, the greater the vegetation, the lower the likelihood of erosion.

Densely Wooded	1 point
Scattered trees and Shrubs	2 points
Grassy with scattered perennials	5 points
Sparse, Sprawling and/or Annual Coverage	8 points

Type of Soil

The structure, density, and size of a soil's particles influence its likelihood of erosion (refer to chapter 3 to determine your type of soil).

Soil dominant in clay, with silt, sand, and organic matter mixed	*1 point*
Sandy soil mixed with silt and organic matter	*2 points*
Clay soil with little or no organic matter	*4 points*
Sandy soil with little or no organic material.	*6 points*

Amount and Type of Activity

People can dramatically alter the power and direction of water by neglecting drainage systems, improperly clearing a landscape, and practicing poor grading techniques. Tunneling animals, such as gophers, ground squirrels, and mice, are a threat to soil stability as well.

Animals and people gently walking	*1 point*
Storm drains clogged / tunneling and browsing animals	*3 points*
An area that was cleared and never replanted	*4 points*
A barren landscape	*6 points*

When you have completed the four sub-categories, add up the scores for a total that estimates the risk of erosion on your property. The list below gives a rough approximation. Methods for reducing runoff and topsoil loss on slopes are discussed at the end of the chapter.

Approximate Level of Risk for Erosion and Topsoil Loss

5–11 points = Moderately low
12–18 points = Medium
19–26 points = Moderately high
27–36 points = High

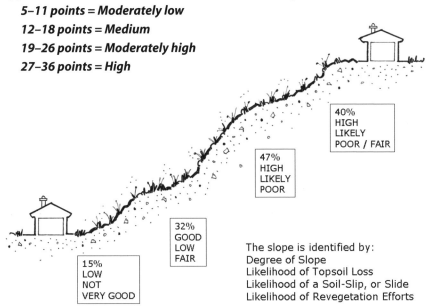

40%
HIGH
LIKELY
POOR / FAIR

47%
HIGH
LIKELY
POOR

32%
GOOD
LOW
FAIR

15%
LOW
NOT
VERY GOOD

The slope is identified by:
Degree of Slope
Likelihood of Topsoil Loss
Likelihood of a Soil-Slip, or Slide
Likelihood of Revegetation Efforts

A slope will rarely have the same degree of incline, or same type of soil, which greatly influences the chances of erosion and your ability to establish hill-holding plants.

Areas for Absorbing Water
A safe and efficient place for infiltration on a slope will possess certain characteristics:
- The infiltration area should be on slopes no greater than 20%.
- A steep, or moderately steep slope should not sit downhill of the infiltration area.
- The infiltration area should be easy to get to and maintain. Sediment, delivered by both wind and water, will fill these depressions.
- The retention area will provide a safe drainage option for overflowing water.
- And lastly, the area should be able to support vigorous vegetation, in order to rapidly wick the water from the soil and increase its capacity to hold more.

Areas for Screening Water
The runoff from slopes will be loaded with debris and sediment. There are devices that filter the water, preventing much of the debris and sediment from entering the storm water system. For a list of screening devices refer to chapter 11. The characteristics of an area suitable for screening include:
- The device should be the furthest device downhill, the last thing the water runs into before leaving the property.
- The area should have good accessibility, because it will need to be regularly cleaned.
- The area should be large enough to support an overflow device, which may be needed in heavy rains, or when the screening device becomes clogged.

CONTROLLING EROSION AND TOPSOIL LOSS
Included in this section are methods and materials that can help you protect an area from erosion. The bulk of the recommendations revolve around the three Ds: Diverting, Draining and De-powering water.

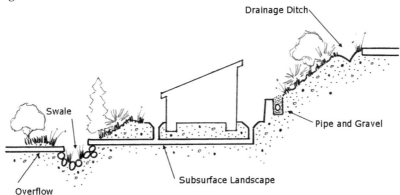

Moving Water Safely Through a Property

Method / Material	Risk	Costs	Maintenance
Bales: *Oat, barley, wheat, and rice straw bales used to slow water and catch sediment*	*Low to high*	*Low*	*May become home for a variety of animals.*
Check Dams: *Boards or rocks used in gullies to stop debris and sediment.*	*Moderate to high*	*Low to moderate*	*Debris will back up against material and need to be hauled away.*
Dry Walls: *Small rock or sandbag walls used to channel and slow water.*	*Moderate to high*	*Moderate*	*Sediment will accumulate on uphill side.*
Concrete Ditches: *Diverts water away from risky areas.*	*Moderate to high*	*High*	*Cleaned before start of rain.*
Fiber Rolls: *Straw, rice hulls, and even coconut waste bound by plastic netting.*	*Low to moderate*	*Low*	*Will be nearly decomposed in two years.*
French Drains: *Trenches filled with gravel wrapped in filter cloth.*	*Low to high*	*Moderate to high*	*If regularly used, they will fail, and need to be dug up and cleaned.*
Matting: *Organic or inorganic mesh laid over the top of soil.*	*Low to high*	*Low to moderate*	*Organic mesh will break down in two years.*
Mulch: *Used to protect soil from water, wind and sun.*	*Low to moderate*	*Low to moderate*	*Re-apply once every two years in exposed areas.*
Planting: *Long term solution.*	*Low to high*	*Low to high*	*Ideally, the plants selected are low maintenance.*
Swales: *A planted ditch used to slow and channel water.*	*Low to moderate*	*Moderate to high*	*Swales will fill over time and need to be cleaned and deepened every three years.*
Terracing: *Walls that demand a cut or fill.*	*Low to moderate*	*High*	*Low maintenance.*

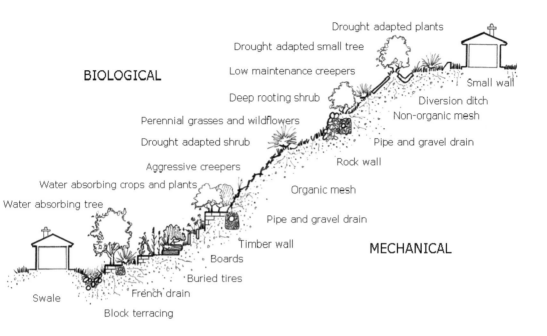

BIOLOGICAL

Drought adapted plants
Drought adapted small tree
Low maintenance creepers
Deep rooting shrub
Perennial grasses and wildflowers
Drought adapted shrub
Aggressive creepers
Water absorbing crops and plants
Water absorbing tree

Small wall
Diversion ditch
Non-organic mesh
Pipe and gravel drain
Rock wall
Organic mesh
Pipe and gravel drain
Timber wall
Boards
Buried tires
French drain
Block terracing
Swale

MECHANICAL

Illustrated above are some of the many biological and mechanical devices that can be employed to reduce runoff and soil erosion.

SCREEN AND CLEAN

Screening and cleaning runoff are important components of a slope practicing CPR. The details of infiltration basins, constructed wetlands, and catch basins are discussed in depth in Chapter 11.

TIPS

Make it Stick: Not only is work on slopes risky and tricky, it is also expensive. Thoroughly examining and planning; spending the money for quality materials; and spending the time to do it right will significantly lower the risk and costs.

Irrigation: Slopes are not nearly as forgiving as flat landscape and over or under watering can have a large effect – from loss of plants to topsoil loss. The elements of an irrigation system that can successfully irrigate your slope are covered in Chapter 4.

Terracing: Although it can be effective, terracing is a labor intensive and expensive method of stabilizing a slope and deceasing erosion and topsoil loss. A soil erosion and sediment control specialist should be consulted prior to initiating any large-scale terracing project.

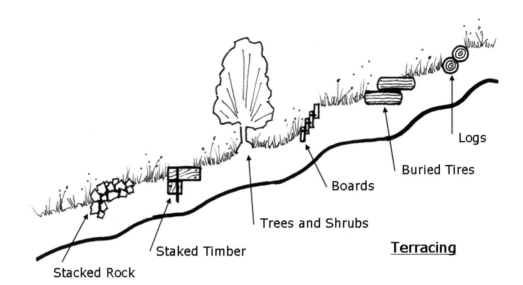

Logs

Buried Tires

Boards

Trees and Shrubs

Terracing

Staked Timber

Stacked Rock

13

CHAPTER THIRTEEN

Fertilizers

The nutrient-rich water running off fertilized properties poses a real threat to the health of our oceans and watersheds. Primarily containing nitrogen and phosphorus compounds, this runoff causes the rapid growth of algae, which in turn degrades fisheries and water clarity. Unfortunately, some vast areas of our ocean are now experiencing "algal blooms" that rob the water of oxygen and kill off our precious marine life. Keeping a landscape and its plants healthy, while reducing nutrient-laden runoff, is the goal of this chapter.

In many cases, store-bought fertilizers are not needed. There are more than enough nutrients cycling through a landscape and home that can be converted into fertilizers. These homemade, organic, low-impact fertilizers have four big benefits over chemicals: They help feed the soil, which improves the health of the entire landscape; they release fewer nutrients to water than chemical fertilizers, improving runoff; they don't over-stimulate plants like many "enhanced" fertilizers, which reduces long-term maintenance costs; and finally, some store-bought fertilizers are petroleum-based products – and the manufacturing process is unnecessarily harmful to the environment.

STEPS
Determine nutrient needs
Examine all options
Make organic fertilizer

USING LESS AND USING ORGANICS
Minerals are needed to drive the life systems in plants. These minerals are called nutrients, and when they are deficient in the soil, a plant will show signs of poor health.

Soil will lose nutrients as a plant absorbs them, or when water pushes them past a plant's root zone (leaching). Also, there are times when these nutrients are in the soil, but the plants cannot absorb them. When a soil is either too alkaline or too acidic, some of these minerals become bound and unavailable for plants to absorb. Plants grown in soils that are low in organic matter, compacted, and/or overwatered may show signs of nutrient deficiencies, when in fact the nutrients are simply unavailable.

When fertilizing is done right, just enough nutrients are provided to meet the needs of the landscape, but not enough to readily run off a landscape during rain. Finding this balance means juggling the quantity of fertilizer used and the frequency of its use. The best times to fertilize are in late summer, well before the fall and winter rains and snow, then again in early spring, to help the landscape in its stage of greatest growth. If there is not a visible reason to fertilize, then don't. Many plants, particularly Mediterranean plants, respond poorly to over-rich soils.

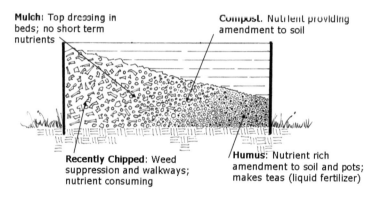

The debris your garden produces can be used throughout your landscape. The illustration above shows the transformation of greenwaste, from recently chipped material, to mulch, compost, and then humus (the most decomposed and richest in nutrients).

IDENTIFYING NUTRIENT DEFICIENCIES

Although identifying nutrient deficiencies can be tough, it helps in protecting against over-fertilization. Not all nutrients are needed all the time. The time of year, changes in environment, stage of plant growth, and the fact that deficiencies may affect plants differently -- all conspire to make identification difficult. The nutrients listed below are needed for plant health, and soil deficiencies will show up in recognizable signs.

Primary Nutrients

These nutrients are the ones most needed by all plants.

Nitrogen: Needed for leaf development. A plant's need for nitrogen is the greatest when it is actively growing. Signs of deficiency include light green leafs, yellowing of older leaves; stunted, weak growth; and underdeveloped leaves. Notably, too much nitrogen can also be harmful to a plant, leading to an abundance of foliage, but not much root, flower, or fruit. The signs of nitrogen loading are dark green leaves and the rapid growth of foliage. Excess nitrogen in a plant can also lead to a variety of pest infestations.

Phosphorus: Needed for the development of cells and the promotion of the transfer of energy throughout a plant. Signs of deficiency include retarded and stunted growth, less fruit than usual, dark or blue/green coloration of leaves, and some plants' leaves may begin to turn purple. Signs occur in older leaves first. Too much phosphorus is not readily apparent, but may cause deficiency in copper and zinc.

Potassium (potash): Helps regulate water in cells, and protects a plant from the effects of heat and cold. Signs of deficiency include weak stems, reduced growth of flower and fruit, and spotted and/or curled older leaves. Older leaves show the signs of deficiency first. Excessive potassium is not usually absorbed by plants, however, it may cause a deficiency in magnesium, manganese, zinc, and possibly iron.

Secondary Nutrients

Not all other nutrients are listed in this section. Some of those not mentioned will probably never be deficient in a soil. Others may not have readily visible indicators of deficiency (unless the plant is closely examined), and the effects may vary greatly between types of plants. The secondary nutrients listed below (commonly called micronutrients) not only have signs of deficiency in plants, but a deficiency may be common.

Calcium: Needed for cell wall development. Signs of deficiency develop in newer leaves first, which become distorted, small, and spotted, and eventually die back.

Magnesium: An important part of the chlorophyll and required for activation of many enzymes. Signs of deficiency include chlorosis (yellowing leaves with green veins), typically spotted on older leaves first (unlike iron deficiency); and tips or margins of leafs are curled upwards.

Iron: A required part of the chlorophyll and help in the processes of photosynthesis and respiration. It also activates other enzymes. Signs of deficiency are similar to those of magnesium, chlorosis (yellowing leaves with green veins), but is visible on the new growth first. Too much iron will be seen as irregular areas of dead tissue in mature leaves (necrotic).

Zinc: Required in the formation of acids. Not usually deficient in soils with a high organic content, but is common in those that are degraded and alkaline. Signs of deficiency include spots growing between the veins of leafs and distance between leafs on stalks will shorten.

Manganese: Helps activate the enzymes responsible for the formation of DNA and RNA. Also helps in the plant's production of oxygen. Manganese is commonly deficient in soils with high organic content, yet alkaline. Signs of deficiency include spots of dead tissue on leafs (while the veins remain green), slow growth, and yellowing of older leaves.

ORGANIC FERTILIZERS

There are two types of organic fertilizers: those that can be made from products found or grown in and around a home, and those that are store-bought. Naturally, the fertilizers created from home are better for the environment; they pull debris from the waste stream and relieve a gardener from having to import the materials. Another strategy for adding minerals to a garden is to grow particular plants, such as those capable of fixating nitrogen (refer to www.surfrider.org/ofg), or those grown as annuals and tilled into the soil, called green manure.

Homemade Fertilizers

Below is a short list of the materials found in a home and recommendations for their use. It should be noted that some of these materials may take some time to decompose and release their stored nutrients.

Aquarium Water: Straight from the fish tank to the garden, aquarium water is high in nitrogen and phosphorus.

Bone Meal: High in phosphorus, bone meal supports flower production, and helps deter some pests, such as ants. Clean the bones from steak or fish, dry them in a microwave, crush them with a mallet in a bag, and then spread and scratch the powder into the soil.

Catch / Infiltration Basin Sludge: Catch basins and retention areas will eventually fill with sediment and debris, and will need to be cleaned out. This sediment is loaded with a variety of nutrients and can either be mixed right into planter beds or added to a compost pile.

Coffee Grounds: This abundant and often-discarded resource is a good source of nitrogen and can be used as light mulch. When added to compost piles, coffee grounds also help produce nitrogen-rich humus. If asked, local coffee houses will typically give a customer their used grounds.

Compost: Along with the debris produced from a landscape, an actively working compost pile can absorb a variety of oddities, such as hair and dry dog food.

Compost Tea: An organic concoction that concentrates nutrients in a liquid form. Useful in overcoming degraded areas and supporting productive landscapes. Tea is made by filling a permeable bag, like nylon stocking or burlap bag, with compost (generally made from worm castings, manures, and/or grass clippings) and setting the bag in a large bucket of water. The tea takes frequent stirring, or mechanical aeration, and about 2 days of seeping.

Eggshells: Containing a large amount of calcium and moderate amount of nitrogen, eggshells can either be scattered directly over a landscape, or put in a compost pile.

Feathers: While not an abundant resource unless there is a bird in a house (or the property has a cat) feathers are an excellent source of nitrogen. This resource should be composted.

Grass Clippings: The debris created from mowing a lawn is a perfect high-nitrogen fertilizer if it is cured in a compost pile first. Scattering freshly cut grass over soil does not work as well, because if it is not kept moist then the sun will chemically break them down and they will be blown off the property; on the other hand, if the clippings are kept too moist, they may produce an acidic barrier on top of the soil.

Hair: Human and pet hair is rich in iron, manganese, and sulphur. Hair is best used as an additive in a compost pile, but when used as mulch it can help deter larger pests, such as some rodents and birds.

Kitchen Scraps: Kitchen scraps of vegetables and fruits make some of the richest composts. Kitchen scraps are fleshy, moist, and loaded with nutrients, which speeds the decomposition process and time required to turn the scraps into compost and humus. Tea bags, coffee grounds, crushed and dry dog food, and eggshells can be thrown into this mix. These high-activity compost piles do not require a lot of room, just an area comparable to an old bathtub; yet they provide an excellent source of readily available nutrients. Kitchen scraps are typically high in phosphorus and potassium, but low in nitrogen (unlike animal products).

Pine Needles: An abundant resource in many landscapes, pine needles belong in a compost pile, or used as a mulch to deter weeds. Needles are low in nitrogen, phosphorus and potassium.

Tea Grounds: An abundant resource in many homes and coffee houses. Tea grounds have a moderate amount of nitrogen and low amounts of phosphorus and potassium. This resource should be composted.

Wood Ashes: Completely cooled and dispersed straight from the fireplace to the garden beds, wood ashes are high in potassium, with minor amounts of phosphorus, which is perfect for flowering and fruiting plants. Ashes are a good addition to the compost pile.

Store-Bought Organic Fertilizers

Store-bought organic fertilizers are listed below, and evaluated on the nutrients they most possess.

Blood Meal: High in nitrogen, low in phosphorus and potassium

Bone Meal: Moderate in nitrogen and high in phosphorus

Chicken Manure: Moderate in nitrogen, high in phosphorus, and moderate in potassium

Cocoa Shell Meal: Moderate in nitrogen, phosphorus and potassium

Corn Gluten: High in nitrogen; inhibits seeds from sprouting

Cottonseed Hull Ash: High in potassium

Cottonseed Meal: High in phosphorus

Fish Meal: High nitrogen and phosphorus and low in potassium

Granite Dust: Moderate in potassium

Greensand: Low in phosphorus and moderate in potassium

Guano: High in nitrogen and moderate in phosphorus

Hoof and Horn Meal: High in nitrogen and low in phosphorus

Phosphate Rock: High in phosphorus

Poultry Manure: Low in nitrogen, moderate in phosphorus and potassium

Sawdust: Low in nitrogen, phosphorus and potassium

Seaweed: Low in nitrogen and moderate in potassium

Steer manure: Moderate in nitrogen, phosphorus and potassium

Two Effective, All-Purpose, Ready to Use, Easy-to-Make Fertilizers

Try one of these two easy-to-whip-up organic fertilizers.

4 parts coffee grounds	*2 parts blood meal*
1 part bone meal	*1 part phosphate rock*
1 part wood ashes	*4 parts wood ashes*

CARING FOR LAWNS

A chemically-maintained lawn is by far the most polluting type of ground cover. Lawns have a variety of disadvantages: They consume the most resources (fossil fuels, water, fertilizers, and pesticides); because of the small-engine tools used to maintain them, they contribute to particulate air pollution and regional air-quality problems; and grass clipping are commonly found in gutters, waiting for rains and wind to push them to the ocean.

However, lawns provide an incredible surface that is nearly impossible to duplicate. If a lawn is used for kids, or athletes, their expense can be justified. Luckily, there are many strategies that can be employed to reduce the negative impacts of lawns.

- Yearly de-thatching and aeration will significantly increase the permeability and health of a lawn. To properly dethatch, mow your lawn shorter than usual and use a sturdy rake to pull the dead material out of it. The lawn should be raked in two separate directions. Aeration involves a manual or engine-driven tool that pulls small plugs from the lawn. The holes left by the aerator are then filled by raking in mulch.

- Yearly mulching and amending will sustain a beautiful lawn without the use of chemicals. The type of mulch used should be the most decomposed, called humus. Amendments good for a lawn are blood meal, chicken manure, coffee grounds, corn gluten, cottonseed meal, and wood ashes. Apply about an inch of humus mixed with amendments and then rake it into the soil and holes left by the aerator.

- Do not commit yourself to a weekly mowing. Instead, plan on mowing only when the grass gets to a predetermined height, such as two and a half inches. Mowing a lawn when it needs it, rather than a weekly schedule, can significantly decrease the frequency of mowing. Leaving the grass leaves at two and a half inches will help keep the soil cool and

moist while reducing shock to the plant.
- Design the shape of a lawn area to the type of sprinkler planning to be used, so that there is no overspray and runoff.
- If using chemical fertilizers, then fertilize early enough to avoid the fall and winter rains/snow, and then again, only after the last of the spring rains have passed. Never fertilize before a storm.
- Put grass clippings in a compost pile. Leaving the grass clippings on top of a lawn after being mowed is not the most efficient way to get the nitrogen locked inside the leaves back to the soil. The blades of grass are wafer thin and rapidly break down, both chemically and biologically. If the clippings do not have direct contact with the soil, they will more likely break down chemically (under the sun), and will be blown off the property, eventual settling in a waterway. Instead, put all grass clippings into a compost pile, let it turn into humus, and then liberally apply it to the lawn after aerating.

TIPS

No Lawn Along Perimeter: Water pouring off a sidewalk and into the storm drain system is a common site in urban communities. Most of this problem can be fixed by putting a two-foot buffer of low-water-using plants between the lawn and your driveway, sidewalk or street. Overspray will water the planted area and not the hardscape.

Notes

CHAPTER FOURTEEN

Weeding Naturally

Weeds can be an unwanted nuisance. But commonly used herbicides are costly, both ecologically and economically. Manufacturing these products consumes a lot of energy, they possess many human health effects, and they are expensive.

Herbicides are not necessary in an established, residential landscape. There are low impact methods of controlling unwanted weeds. This chapter will not only help you control the weeds currently onsite, but help in protecting a site from weeds in the future.

STEPS
Tackle weeds on the three levels.

PRVENTION, PROTECTION, ERADICATION

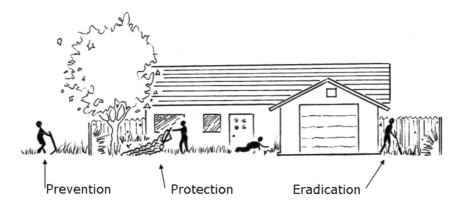

Prevention   Protection   Eradication

Prevention prevents the weeds from coming in, protection stops the weed from taking root, and eradication removes the weed once established.

Prevention

Preventing weeds from blowing onto your property is the most cost effective technique for weed control.

Barriers: Weed seeds are brought into a landscape by the wind, birds, and people. The seeds coming in on the wind can be reduced by planting or building barriers. A barrier can be a thick, aggressive shrub, like ceanothus, juniper, or rosemary; or a small wall made from stone or recycled concrete.

No Seed: Never let the weeds on your property go to seed. If the weeds are high, like grasses, then mow or weed whack them. If the weeds are low, like bindweed and spurge, then drag a hoe over the top of them and cut the plant at its base.

Look Outward: Simply putting up barriers and weeding your own property may not be enough to stop the constant migration of weed seeds. Sometimes, your efforts will be needed in the landscapes outside of your own. Removing weeds from adjacent properties or creating a buffer zone around your own property can reduce the amount of time needed to weed your landscape.

Protection

Weed seeds will inevitably get onto your property -- and protective measures will help ensure that they never take root.

A Healthy Landscape: Cliché or not, the best defense against weeds is a good offense. Design and maintain a landscape that is capable of competing with and beating weeds for available space. Plants are adapted to your climate, soils, and other conditions – making them great competitors in the garden.

Mulches: Controlling weeds by using mulches is a universally recommended method of control, and by far the best. Mulch suppresses growth by blanketing existing weeds, or robbing seeds the opportunity to touch soil and root. Not all mulches are equally effective though. Recently chipped acacia, eucalyptus, juniper, and pittosporum are the best, because they contain chemicals that inhibit germination. Large, thick mulches are preferred over fine, thin mulches.

Soil/Weed Barriers: Weed cloth, newspaper, and plastic can be used as a barrier over the top of soil to prevent weeds from rooting. Cloth and newspaper barriers are permeable and preferred. However, if not mulched and protected, most barriers will break down and become ineffective within two years.

Corn Gluten Meal: Although not commonly used, this remedy is an organic alternative to herbicides. Corn gluten has chemicals that inhibit the growth of seeds. Spread 20 pounds over 1,000 square feet. However, it may not be effective the first year and may need yearly applications for 2 to 3 years.

Eradication

All gardens have weeds and there are a variety of methods to eradicate them.

Hand Pulling: Touring your garden every two weeks in spring and early summer and pulling the weeds in their first few weeks of life is the simplest, cheapest, and most effective form of weed control. New shoots are easy to pull, and most are good for a compost pile. Hand pulling is a quick, easy task if done regularly.

Sheet Mulching: Laying four to six inches of mulch over the top of weeds will most likely kill them. With the exceptions of Bermuda grass and ivy, few plants can survive such an extensive smothering.

Tilling: Constantly turning the weeds in your landscape into the ground will not only kill the weed and prevent it from going to seed, but it will also enrich the soil.

Vinegar: This acidic solution is a contact killer that can be used straight, or diluted with water up to 50%. However, it only kills what it touches and will not kill the roots of re-sprouting weeds, such as Bermuda grass and bramble.

Chapter 5: The methods prescribed for reclaiming a landscape from turf can be used to reclaim small areas. This chapter also has a list ways to use herbicides effectively.

Notes

CHAPTER FIFTEEN

Pests

*Every landscape has pests: unwanted weeds, insects,
and animals. How you perceive and manage these
pests determines, in part, the amount of pesticides swept off
your property. Gardeners practicing CPR may be more
tolerant of some pests, may change the composition
of their landscapes to deter particularly
destructive and determined pests, or may seek less
toxic alternatives for eliminating others.*

Pesticides are swept off our properties during periods of rain and over-irrigation. These pesticides pose a significant threat to aquatic life and groundwater supplies. According to the US Environmental Protection Agency, diazinon and chlorpyrifos are the two most common pesticides found in our water – both of which are classified as posing a "very high" risk to aquatic invertebrates. Other pesticides that pose a risk, and were detected in residential runoff, are carbamates, soaps, oils, malathion, botanical insecticides, pyrethroids, insect growth regulators, and microbials.

This chapter follows the same path in pest management that was created by California's Cooperative Extension, called Integrated Pest Management (IPM). IPM employs easy-to-use strategies instead of harmful chemicals.

Organized by type of pest (insects, animals and fungi), each section below provides biological, cultural, physical, and homemade remedies to control those common pests.

STEPS
Determine type of pest
Organize a strong offense
Attack a pest with least toxic alternative first.

INSECTS

Using chemical insecticides/pesticides is not the first line of defense in a landscape practicing CPR. Many pesticides can kill or harm beneficial organisms, such as birds, animals, aquatic species, and beneficial insects. Pesticides can also affect the health of humans. Luckily, effective yet ecologically benign alternatives exist, such as soap sprays. *When a soap spray is recommended as a remedy, as it often is with soft-bodied insects, do not use antibacterial soaps.* Bacteria in soil is natural and essential to healthy plants and environments.

The methods gardeners use to care for their garden can influence the type and amount of pests. Overcrowding, unhealthy plants, poor air circulation, over-fertilization, and improper watering can all lead to a landscape more susceptible to particular insects. An unkempt and cluttered landscape is also more susceptible to particular pests. The insects most likely to be a problem are listed below. Each listing provides alternative strategies for controlling the insect, plants that can be grown to deter the insect, and any cultural practices that encourage the insect.

ATTRACTING BENEFICIAL INSECTS

Insecticides are as unwanted in an ocean or lake as they are in a garden – they generally kill everything. Beneficial insects are needed instead, those that devour the bugs eating your favorite plant. Braconid wasps, hover flies, lady beetles, lacewings, and tachinid flies will respond to your call if you provide the three basic requirements: food, water and habitat.

Beneficial insects also need nectar and pollen to thrive. A wide variety of small, easily accessible flowers blooming throughout the year will provide a rich source of alternate food. The plants that produce these flowers are usually either native, or come from the aster, carrot, or mint families (refer to www.surfrider.org/ofg for specifics). A small bird bath, or water fountain, will provide water. And habitat is provided by covering bare dirt with mulch, or creating fairly dense shrubby areas, like hedgerows.

Ants: Barriers such as sticky tape and roofing tar are good to keep ants out of trees and shrubs (where they can distribute and protect aphids and mealy bugs for their dew). Lemon juice is a good deterrent when poured in the cracks ants will occupy or travel. Spearmint sprays (spearmint pureed, strained, and then added to 2 parts water) and soap sprays (1 to 4 tablespoons per gallon of water) are good deterrents. Diatomaceous earth works well, too. Plant pennyroyal, spearmint, southernwood, or tansy to repel ants.

Aphids: Since aphids are attracted to nitrogen-rich, humid environments, reduce the use of fertilizers and water, and prune plants to allow air circulation to reduce moisture. Rubbing leaves together with fingers is surest method of control. A jet of water can dislodge them. The best homemade remedy is a soap spray (1 to 4 tablespoons per gallon of water), but others include teas with a combination of tobacco stem, onion, garlic and shallot. Simply controlling ants can reduce the aphid population. Place garlic at the base of infected plants. Plant angelica, chives, garlic, mustards, nasturtium, onions, petunias, southernwood, or spearmint as repellents. Ladybugs devour aphids.

Black Widow Spiders: These venomous spiders prefer dark and cool environments, such as wood piles, dry-stacked walls, and the clutter of a garden. Remove debris and clutter from around the house.

Cockroaches: Well suited to the urban environment, these decomposers can be found almost anywhere. Clean and store stuff away from home. Caulk cracks and protect small openings into the house with a screen. Boric acid is a good repellent, and there are maze-like traps that work with no chemicals.

Cutworm: Till and turn over infected beds, or spread cornmeal across the area and cutworms will die from indigestion. Lay mulches of eggshells, wood ashes, chicken manure, and oak leaves around new plants. Cut back wild grasses in fall, where moths lay their eggs. A 2-inch aluminum collar wrapped around the base of a plant may deter them. Plant tansy.

Fleas: As the temperature goes up, so does the flea population. Besides regularly vacuuming your house and washing/combing your pet, there are a variety of remedies. Fleas hate Eucalyptus -- so place the tree's leafs in jars and nylon stockings around the house and garden. Eucalyptus leafs and bark also makes great mulch. Place a bowl full of soapy water under a light to attract and drown fleas at night. Place 8 thinly sliced lemons in a gallon bucket, fill with boiling water, let the mixture sit overnight, and then spray liberally on your pet to help repel fleas. Finally, beneficial nematodes will devour fleas.

Hives: Not all the hives of flying insects are bad. Yellow jackets and paper wasps are considered beneficial insects, because they eat house flies and other pests. Prevention is the best method of control; screen all openings and cracks with wire mesh 1/8 inch or smaller. Dislodge new hives with a jet of water. Call professionals if the hive and colony is large. Mint oil is a good repellent against wasps and hornets.

Mealybugs: These insects thrive in warm and humid environments. Dry the area and prune to improve air circulation. A jet of water to the undersides of leaves dislodges the insects. Cotton swaps dampened with rubbing alcohol and swiped across leaves will kill them. A mixture of dish soap and water is an effective deterrent too, as is kerosene and water (both mixtures are 1 to 4 tablespoons per gallon of water). Control the ants that help distribute them.

Mites: These tiny bugs are attracted to a dusty, humid environment. Water-stressed plants are more susceptible too. Wash foliage with a stream of water, let the area dry, and make sure the plants are properly watered. Soap sprays and neem oil are effective controls, as well as capsaicin (hot pepper sauce) and water (1 to 4 tablespoons per gallon of water).

Mosquito: Mosquitoes breed in stagnant water, even small amounts, such as in the crevices of the leaves. Naturally, remove stagnant water. Citronella is good repellent. Plant ageratum, basil, catnip, marigold, or rosemary. Rosemary and catnip can be rubbed directly on clothes, or made into a tea and sprayed on clothes and skin.

Pine Beetles: A somewhat serious problem across North America, this beetle attacks unhealthy and weakened pines. There is no real effective chemical control. Remove infested trees in winter (when the beetles are less active and likely to flee), prune damaged branches as you spot them, increase distance between trees, and deeply water trees in the long, dry summer months.

Scale: Like mites (which they are related to), scale thrive in dusty, humid environments. Wash both sides of the foliage with a jet of water and dry the area. Maintain healthy plants. Scrape or wipe bugs off with a cloth dipped in alcohol or turpentine. Horticultural oil and dormant sprays are effective in spring and summer. Control the ants that help distribute them.

Snails and Slugs: Remove high grasses, weeds, and piles of debris. A good trap is beer or grape juice in a pie pan buried at soil level. Another effective trap is to create a welcoming home for them by stacking moist wood to create a protected shelter and in the afternoon, when they are hiding, they can be easily picked out. Copper strips provide a good barrier, but may be short lived. Protect the base of plants with anything coarse, such as used sandpaper, berry bramble, oak leaves, diatomaceous earth, or wood ashes. A tea made from wormwood can repel them. Plant prostrate rosemary and wormwood.

Spider Mites: Spider mites are attracted to plants with leaves high in nitrogen. They spread easily if plants are grown too close together. Remove or prune plants to create more open, breezy space. Apply dormant spray or horticultural oil to deciduous plants in spring. Spray a mixture of ground limestone and dish soap if infestation gets bad. Plant chives, garlic, or onions.

Thrips: A widely distributed pest that prefers flowers and fruit. Mowing wild weeds helps enormously. A mixture of canola oil and water is a good repellent; or tobacco juice, oil, and water; or a paste of 1 part yeast, 1 part sugar mixed with water and smeared on flower buds. Attract green lacewings, as they will eat thrips.

Whiteflies: These insects are common in humid environments with poor air circulation. Prune plants and open the area to air circulation. Sticky tape will trap them and jets of water will dislodge them, both of which are the surest remedies. Teas made from tobacco are also effective in sprays, and dust made from tobacco is a good repellent. Ladybugs will eat whiteflies. Plant marigolds, nasturtium, or tree tobacco as a deterrent.

ANIMALS

Cats: To deter cats from using the garden beds as a restroom, lay thick, woody mulches over the area. Palm fronds over sand boxes will provide a shield. Spread powders made of cayenne pepper; black pepper; or flour, mustard, cayenne, and chili powder over beds. Some claim that orange and lemon peels are effective deterrents. Plant chives, garlic, or onions.

Deer: Not a pest to everybody. Keep out of the garden with fences and barriers. Protect individual plants with chicken wire if planted in an open area. Dogs are sometimes good deterrents. Plant deer-resistant plants, which tend to have small, resinous, brittle leaves. Deterrents include soap bars and hair hanging in branches, and mixtures of garlic, capsaicin (hot pepper sauce), peppermint, and rotting eggs.

Dogs: Deter a dog with its nose. Dried and crushed red peppers or cayenne powder spread around the areas visited are effective deterrents. Thorny ground covers and mulches work as deterrents too. Plant chives, garlic, or onions.

Gophers: These herbivores can do a lot of damage to a landscape. Traps are the most effective remedy. Shove castor beans and elderberry branches in their holes and runs. Every method of control requires diligence and repeated efforts.

Moles: These diggers tend to do more damage in heavily watered gardens. Let the soil dry. Cram a variety of items in the outlets and runs, including garlic, human hair, moth crystals, thorny stems, elderberry leafs and stems, caster oil or seeds, rotten eggs, and hot peppers. Visit the area daily and keep shoving the repellents back in their holes. Traps are the surest remedy.

Rabbits: These critters are common in urban developments bordering natural areas. Dogs and cats are good deterrents. Lay coarse mulches, such as recently chipped trees, eggshells, and bramble around new and vulnerable plantings. Mulches of pepper sauce, daffodil bulbs, iris rhizomes, catnip, and spearmint may work as well. Plant anything in the onion family, such as chives, garlic, or onions. As with deer, fencing is the surest way to protect particular plants or areas within a landscape.

Skunks: Although feared by humans, skunks are good for a garden. They have a diverse appetite and eat fallen fruit, bugs, beetles, and mice, all of which can be pests in a garden. If necessary, get rid of their homes by cleaning or removing wood piles, cleaning drainage pipes, and routing out other small hiding spots. Make sure the lids of trash-cans are on tight.

OPOSSUMS: A GARDENER'S HELPER

Bloated, rat-like, tiny feet, long scaly tail – opossums are scary looking creatures, but it's a façade. These scavengers are hardly fierce and perform many handy chores when you're fast asleep. Opossums will eat snails, slugs and cockroaches. Because of their lower than usual body temperature, they are, luckily, fairly rabies resistant. Opossums are poor climbers and will rarely go into a tree to get fruit, preferring the stuff that's fallen. Opossums are garden contributors. Notably – snail bait can harm these useful animals.

FUNGI

Of the four types of pesticides (herbicides, insecticides, rodenticides, and fungicides) fungicides do the most damage to the aquatic environment, and some are known to kill fish. Fungi prefer moist, humid, warm environments. The likelihood of a fungus spreading and causing damage increases with the presence of other pests, such as mealy bugs, scale, and boring insects (which provides access to the inside of a plant).

Some of the homemade sprays used against fungi include 2 teaspoons of baking soda and 1 to 2 teaspoons of fine-grade horticultural oil mixed with 1 gallon of water; 1 part milk to 9 parts water on the plants (milk can also be a foliar fertilizer); 1 part mouthwash to 9 parts water; and 2 tablespoons of bleach and 2 tablespoons of baby shampoo in 1 gallon of water. Notably, mouthwash can not be considered organic.

Black Spot: A disease that causes black spots and yellow margins on leaves, which will eventually fall off. When watering, try to keep the leaves dry; prune the plants to increase air circulation, and destroy those leaves with the disease. A spray of 6 tablespoons of vinegar to 1 gallon of water may work, but be careful as the vinegar can harm some plants (test first). Another notable spray is 1 teaspoon of baking soda for 1 quart of water, with a few drops of dish soap.

Blight: The term blight refers to a number of diseases usually caused by bacteria and fungi. These diseases prefer moist, humid, and hot environments, and naturally, removing one of the three will help reduce the spread of blight. Cut back on watering and prune to allow sun penetration. Not much can be done for infected plants, except to remove and dispose the infected parts. The spread of disease can also be slowed by deterring the insects that spread it, like aphids. If caught early, try a spray of 2 tablespoons of bleach and 2 tablespoons of baby shampoo in 1 gallon of water.

Powdery Mildew: Increase air circulation and sunlight through pruning and removing plants. A jet of water can dislodge and sometimes kill this fungus. Let the area completely dry afterwards. Prune heavily infected plants and dispose of the vegetation in trash. Sprays include 1 tablespoon of baking soda, 1 to 2 teaspoons of canola oil mixed with 1 gallon of water, or try 3 tablespoons of vinegar to 1 gallon of water.

Root Rots: Root rot is any number of funguses that kill the plant at or below its base (which includes damping off in seedlings). Increase soil drainage with amendments or dramatically cut back on watering. Plant rot-resistant varieties.

Rust: This is common on roses grown along coast. Plant rust-resistant varieties. Increase air circulation and the amount of direct sunlight. Prune heavily infected plants and throw the vegetation in the trash.

Sooty Mold: This very visible pest (it coats leaves with a black, sticky film) is a sign of high humidity and poor air circulation. Wash the foliage off with a jet of water, open the area up with pruning, and let it dry. It is easily spread by aphids, mealy bugs, and whiteflies (see above for controls).

CHAPTER SIXTEEN

Maintaining Permeable Surfaces and Retention Devices

Permeable surfaces will turn impervious over time.
Poorly maintained retention devices will increase the chances
of runoff, erosion, and topsoil loss.

An ocean friendly garden requires maintenance.

Almost like our children, permeable surfaces need your attention, screening and cleaning devices need your time, and retention areas need special consideration. Below are recommendations that will save you time that can be devoted to your children (or other pursuits of happiness).

PERMEABLE SURFACES

Maintenance has two huge affects: it can influence the amount of runoff your landscape produces; and maintenance, or lack thereof, can put debris and toxins in water's path. With these two effects in mind, try employing the following strategies.

Avoid Blowers: Blowers push a property's debris into the air, nearby properties, and the street -- all of which eventually ends up in the ocean. Either avoid the use of blowers, or blow a property's debris away from a street and into a corner where it can be trapped and swept up.

Sweep or Vacuum: The effectiveness of pavers, bricks, turf blocks and other permeable or semi-permeable surfaces, will diminish over time, as fine particles fill the gaps. These special surfaces need a thorough and annual cleaning, preferably with a broom or vacuum, but not a blower. In climates with snow, try reducing the amount of salt and sand used on the surfaces, as these will rapidly fill pore space.

Rake Less Meticulously: In garden beds and areas with exposed soils, try to always leave a little leaf litter to protect the soil from water and wind erosion. Some people find exposed, neatly raked soil appealing, but it is not good for our ocean, soil, or plants.

Water Deeply and Infrequently: Watering not only supplies plants with a life-supporting resource, but also helps a soil exchange its gases. A biologically active soil will require a lot of oxygen, yet the carbon dioxide released by organisms accumulates quickly. Deep watering pushes the carbon dioxide out, and as the soil dries, it pulls oxygen in.

Fix Cow Paths: A cow path is an unintentional footpath on bare soil. People prefer the shortest distance between two points and will oftentimes take this path, even if it means marching through planted beds. Cow paths typically have compacted soil and are quick to produce runoff, which leads to topsoil loss. Either provide a safe, permeable walkway where walkers have identified their preferred path, or install a deterrent to the path's use.

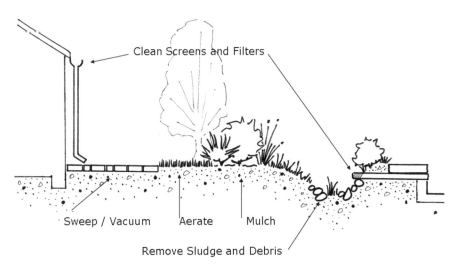

SCREENING, CLEANING & RENTENTION DEVICES

As with anything with a purpose, infiltration, screening, and drainage devices need to be regularly cleaned in order to remain effective. Swales, infiltration basins, and sediment traps should be cleaned every two years, removing the debris and sediment that has accumulated. If the device is permeable, like swales, then they may need to be aerated as well. All these cleaning and aerating tasks should be done after the end of the rainy season, late spring, giving the area plenty of time to recover before the next season. The sediment pulled from these low areas will be loaded with nutrients and can be spread throughout a garden.

Every year the screening devices and storm drain system needs to be cleaned before the start of the rainy season, and depending on the intensity of rain, may have to be periodically cleaned throughout the wet season. Included in these yearly tasks are removing soil away from storm drain grates and protecting them with gravel or matting; examining the drain pipes, looking for debris and breaks (flushing the debris out of the pipes and fixing the breaks). Above-soil screening fabrics may have to be replaced every two to three years.

Importantly, always watch for rills, which are small indents in soils caused by running water. Rills can turn into gullies over time and they represent topsoil loss. Find the source of the running water and direct it to a drainage system.

Notes

Glossary

AQUIFER *An underground formation capable of storing and providing water.*

BIORETENTION *A planted area designed to collect, filter, and/or allow water to infiltrate.*

CATCH BASIN *A below-ground receptacle that allows sediment to drop out before directing the water to a drainage system.*

COMPACTION *The process of making a soil denser, and less permeable.*

CONSTRUCTED WETLAND *An artificially-created wetland used to remove pollutants from runoff and other types of contaminated water. Biological processes remove metals, nutrients and pathogens.*

CONTAMINANT *A substance that when added to water makes the water unfit for consumption and use.*

DETENTION BASIN *Used for the temporary storage of runoff. Called a dry pond if not irrigated.*

DITCH *An open drain running across a slope.*

DRAINAGE *The collection and transportation of water and runoff.*

DRY POND *See detention basin or seasonal pond.*

EMERGENCY SPILLWAY *A channel used to divert overflowing water from retention areas, such as infiltration basins and sediment ponds.*

ERODIBILITY *The likelihood of soil being dislodged and moved.*

EROSION *The separation and transportation of soil particles by water, wind, gravity, and/or activity.*

EVAPOTRANSPIRATION *The loss of water in soil due to evaporation and transpiration (see below).*

FILTERING *The processes of trapping solid particles suspended in water.*

GRAY WATER *Household waste water from tubs, sinks, and washers (but not toilets).*

GROUNDWATER *Water residing within underground rock or soil.*

HYDROZONE *A group of plants that share similar watering needs.*

IMPERMEABLE *A material that does not allow water to pass through it, which can be naturally occurring or manmade.*

INFILTRATION *The flow of water downward, from a land surface to a subsurface.*

INFILTRATION BASIN *An area designated and designed to collect water, allowing it to infiltrate to the soils below.*

IRRIGATION VALVE *A device that allows you to turn an irrigation line on and off, either manually or automatically.*

LEACHING *Pushing solids and nutrients beyond a plant's root zone through the use of water. Leaching can be beneficial, as in getting rid of salts, or it can be harmful, as when nutrients such as nitrogen are leached to aquifers.*

NONPOINT SOURCE POLLUTION *Pollution coming from a large area, but not a specific source. Residential and commercial landscapes are considered nonpoint sources of pollution.*

NON-POTABLE WATER *Water unfit to drink.*

PERMEABLE *A material that allows water to pass through it.*

PH *A measure of alkalinity (greater than 7) or acidity (less than 7), with 7 being neutral pH and 6.5 being ideal for the majority of plants.*

POINT SOURCE POLLUTION *Pollution that has an identifiable source, such as a specific pipe, factory, or event.*

POTABLE WATER *Water fit to drink.*

RECHARGE *Water purposely added to an aquifer.*

RETENTION BASIN *An area designed to capture, filter and (sometimes) infiltrate runoff.*

RETAINING WALL *A wall constructed to prevent soil from moving downward.*

RIPRAP *Stones, and like materials, placed on a slope, in gullies, and around storm drains to help slow erosion.*

RUNOFF *Water that runs over the top of a land surface.*

SEASONAL POND *A designated area used to collect, filter, and infiltrate water from run-off. Sometimes called a vernal pond because it receives no irrigation.*

SEDIMENT *Material that has been moved by water, wind, gravity, or activity.*

SEDIMENT BASIN *A reservoir within a drainage system that slows runoff, allowing the suspended material in the water to drop out.*

WEATHER-BASED IRRIGATION CONTROLLER *A device that automatically turns on irrigation valves based on the plants on the valve and current weather.*

STORM DRAIN *An opening in the ground that captures water and sends it to a storm drain system.*

STORM DRAIN SYSTEM *A system of pipes and devices used to control storm water and protect urban areas from flooding.*

SWALE *A constructed and vegetated channel used to direct, slow, filter, and infiltrate water from runoff.*

TEAS *Nylon stockings stuffed with a variety of organics and allowed to seep in water for 24 to 36 hours. Teas can be used as liquid fertilizers, pest control sprays and compost stimulators.*

TRANSPIRATION *Water released to the atmosphere by the leaves of plants.*

WATERSHED *An area of land, large or small, that drains into one specific place, such as a storm drain outlet, river, or ocean.*

WEEPHOLE *A small hole in a retaining wall that allows water, and excess water pressure, to escape.*